FLASHMAPS
BOSTON

Editor
Robert P. Blake

Creative Director
Fabrizio La Rocca

Cartographer
David Lindroth

Designer
Tigist Getachew

Editorial Contributors
Anne Stuart
Martha Schulman
Steven Amsterdam

Cartographic Contributors
Edward Faherty
Sheila Levin
Page Lindroth
Marcy Pritchard
Eric Rudolph
Gretchen Schmelzer

Contents

PARKS & RECREATION — MAP

SHOPPING — MAP

RESTAURANTS & HOTELS — MAP

NIGHTLIFE — MAP

Special Sales

Fodor's Travel Publications are available at special discounts for bulk purchases for sales promotions or premiums. Special editions, including personalized covers, excerpts of existing guides, and corporate imprints, can be created in large quantities for special needs. For more information, contact your local bookseller or write to Special Markets, Fodor's Travel Publications, 201 East 50th St., New York, NY 10022. Inquiries from Canada should be directed to your local Canadian bookseller or sent to Random House of Canada, Ltd., Marketing Dept., 1265 Aerowood Dr., Mississauga, Ontario L4W 1B9. Inquiries from the United Kingdom should be sent to Fodor's Travel Publications, 20 Vauxhall Bridge Rd., London, England SW1V 2SA. **ISBN 0-679-00007-0**

MANUFACTURED IN THE UNITED STATES OF AMERICA 10 9 8 7 6 5 4 3 2 1

Area Codes: All (617) unless otherwise noted.

EMERGENCIES

Ambulance/Fire/Police ☎ 911

Animal Rescue League ☎ 426-9170

Animal Shelter (MSPCA)
☎ 522-5055

Animal Emergency ☎ 522-7282

Battered Women's Hotline
☎ 661-7203

Child-at-Risk Hotline
☎ 800/792-5200

Children's Aid ☎ 267-3700

Coast Guard ☎ 565-9200

Dental Emergencies & Referrals
☎ 636-6828, 800/917-6453

Drug & Alcohol Hotlines
☎ 445-1500, 624-5111, 800/327-5050

Parental Stress Hotline
☎ 800/632-8188

Poison Information Center
☎ 232-2120, 800/682-9211

Rape Crisis Centers
☎ 492-7273, 442-6300

Suicide Prevention ☎ 247-0220

Traveler's Aid ☎ 542-7286, 737-2880

24-Hour Pharmacy
☎ 876-5519, 282-5246

Visiting Nurse Assn ☎ 800/696-3838

SERVICES

AAA ☎ 800/222-4357

AARP ☎ 723-7600

AIDS Hotline ☎ 800/235-2331

Alcoholics Anonymous ☎ 426-9444

Amex Lost Charge Cards
☎ 800/528-4800

Amex Lost Travelers Checks
☎ 800/221-7282

Attorney General ☎ 727-2200

Better Business Bureau ☎ 426-9000

Birth Certificates ☎ 635-4177

**Black Community Information
Center** ☎ 445-3098

Broken Streetlights ☎ 635-7500

Chamber of Commerce ☎ 227-4500

Citizens Info Service ☎ 727-7030

City Hall Boston ☎ 635-4000

City Hall Cambridge ☎ 349-4000

Consumer Affairs ☎ 727-7780

Convention & Visitor's Bureau
☎ 536-4100

Federal Bureau of Investigation
☎ 742-5533

Garbage Collection ☎ 482-5300

Governor's Office ☎ 727-3600

Handicapped Information
☎ 727-7440, 800/642-0249

Immigration ☎ 565-3879

Internal Revenue Service
☎ 536-1040

Legal Advice or Referrals
☎ 542-9103, 742-9179

Library/Boston Public ☎ 536-5400

**Mass Commission Against
Discrimination** ☎ 727-3990

**Mass Turnpike Road/Weather
Conditions** ☎ 800/828-9104

Mayor's Office ☎ 635-4000

Medicaid
☎ 348-5500, 800/841-2900

Medicare
☎ 800/882-1228

Parking Tickets ☎ 635-4410

Passports ☎ 565-6990

Physician Referral ☎ 726-5800

Planned Parenthood ☎ 738-1370

Postal Service ☎ 654-5001

Public Health ☎ 624-6000

Registry of Motor Vehicles
☎ 351-4500

Snow Removal Boston: ☎ 635-3050,
Cambridge: ☎ 349-4860

Social Security ☎ 800/772-1213

State Police ☎ 508/820-2300

Time of Day ☎ 637-1234, 637-1111

Towaways ☎ 635-3900

Traffic/Road Reports
☎ 374-1234

Travel & Tourism
☎ 727-3201, 800/447-6277

Veteran's Administration
☎ 227-4600

Weather ☎ 936-1234

Zip Code Info ☎ 654-7567

TOURS

Cruises

A C Cruise Line ☎ 261-6633

Bay State Cruise Co ☎ 723-7800

Boston Harbor Cruises ☎ 227-4320

Boston Harbor Whale Watch ☎ 345-9866

Charles River Boat Co ☎ 621-3001

Mass Bay Lines ☎ 542-8000

New England Aquarium ☎ 973-5281

Odyssey Cruises ☎ 654-9700

Spirit of Boston ☎ 457-1450

Sightseeing

Arlington Street Church ☎ 536-7050

Bay Colony Historical Tours ☎ 523-7303

Beacon Hill Gardens ☎ 227-4392

Beantown Trolley ☎ 781/986-6100

Boston By Foot ☎ 367-2345

Boston Duck Tours ☎ 723-3825

Boston Globe ☎ 929-2653

Boston Public Library ☎ 536-5400

Brush Hill Tours ☎ 781/986-6100

Christian Science Center ☎ 450-3790

Discovering Boston ☎ 323-2554

Federal Reserve Bank ☎ 973-3451

Freedom Trail Tours ☎ 635-7412, 242-5642

Gray Lines ☎ 781/986-6100

Historic Boston ☎ 227-4679

Historic Neighborhoods ☎ 426-1885

John Hancock Observatory ☎ 247-1977

Mass Bay Brewing Co ☎ 574-9551

Minuteman Tours ☎ 876-5539

Old State House ☎ 242-5642

Old Town Trolley ☎ 269-7010

Skywalk ☎ 236-3318

Trinity Church ☎ 536-0944

USS *Constitution* ☎ 426-1812

Victorian Society ☎ 267-6338

Whites of Their Eyes ☎ 241-7575

Women's Heritage Trails ☎ 242-5642, 242-5688

TRANSPORTATION

Amtrak ☎ 800/872-7245; 482-3660

Bonanza Bus Terminal ☎ 720-4110

Boston Cab ☎ 262-2227

Boston Cab Assn ☎ 536-5010

Cambridge Yellow Cab ☎ 625-5000

Ferries:

Bay State Cruise Company
Boston to Hull ☎ 723-7800

Hy-Line Ferries
Hyannis to Martha's Vineyard or
Nantucket ☎ 508/778-2600

Massachusetts Bay Lines
Boston to Hingham ☎ 542-8000

Steamship Authority
Woods Hole to Martha's Vineyard
☎ 508/477-8600
Hyannis to Nantucket
☎ 508/771-4000, 508/477-8600

Greyhound Bus Terminal
☎ 526-1801, 800/231-2222

Independent Taxi Operators Assoc ☎ 268-1313

Logan Airport Ground Transportation ☎ 800/235-6426

Logan International Airport
☎ 567-5400

Logan Water Shuttle ☎ 330-8680

Mass Bay Transportation Authority (MBTA: Bus, 'T', Commuter Rail)
☎ 222-3200, 800/392-6100

MBTA Hearing Impaired Information ☎ 222-5415

MBTA Logan Airport
☎ 800/235-6426

MBTA Lost & Found ☎ 222-3200

MBTA Police ☎ 222-1212

MBTA Road Conditions/Weather
☎ 800/828-9104

MBTA Special Needs ☎ 222-5123

Peter Pan Bus Lines ☎ 426-7838

Red & White Cab ☎ 242-8000

PARKS AND RECREATION

Arnold Arboretum ☎ 524-1717

Beaches ☎ 727-5114

Bicycling ☎ 491-7433

Boating ☎ 523-1038

Fishing ☎ 727-3151

Golf Courses:

George Wright, Hyde Park
☎ 361-8313

William Devine, Dorchester
☎ 265-4084

Fresh Pond, Cambridge
☎ 349-6282

Ponkapoag, Canton
☎ 828-4242

Ice Skating ☎ 727-5114

In-Line Skating (rentals) ☎ 482-7400

**Metropolitan District Commission
(MDC)** ☎ 727-5114

Parks & Recreation Info ☎ 635-4505

Racket Sports ☎ 523-9746

**Running: Boston Athletic Assoc
(Boston Marathon)** ☎ 236-1652

Skiing:

Blue Hills ☎ 828-7490
(downhill)

Weston ☎ 781/894-2503
(cross-country)

Swimming ☎ 727-5114

YMCA ☎ 536-7800

YWCA ☎ 351-7600

SPECTATOR SPORTS

Boston Bruins/Hockey ☎ 624-1900

Boston Celtics/Basketball
☎ 523-3030

Boston Marathon ☎ 236-1652

Boston Red Sox/Baseball
☎ 267-8661

Dog Racing/Wonderland
☎ 284-1300

Horse Racing/Suffolk Downs
☎ 567-3900

LPGA/Blue Hills CC ☎ 828-2000

New England Patriots/Football
☎ 800/543-1776

PGA/Pleasant Valley CC
☎ 508/865-4441

Polo/Myopia Hunt Club
☎ 978/468-4433

Tennis/US Pro Longwood
☎ 731-2900

INTERCOLLEGIATE ATHLETICS

Babson ☎ 781/239-4250

Boston College ☎ 552-3000

Boston University ☎ 353-4632

Brandeis ☎ 781/736-3630

Harvard ☎ 495-4848

MIT ☎ 253-4498

Northeastern ☎ 437-2672

Tufts ☎ 627-3232

ENTERTAINMENT

BankBoston Celebrity Series
☎ 482-2595

Berklee Performance Center
☎ 266-7455

BOSTIX ☎ 723-5181

Boston Ballet ☎ 695-6950

Boston Camerata ☎ 262-2092

Boston Lyric Opera ☎ 542-4912

Boston Pops ☎ 266-1492

Boston Symphony Orchestra
☎ 266-1492

Children's Museum ☎ 426-6500

Colonial Theatre ☎ 426-9366

Dance Umbrella Inc ☎ 492-7578

FleetCenter ☎ 624-1000

Franklin Park Zoo/Stone Zoo
☎ 442-4896

Great Woods Ctr ☎ 508/339-2333

Handel & Haydn Society
☎ 266-3605

Harborlights (summer) ☎ 374-9000

Hub Ticket Agency ☎ 426-8340

Movie Fone ☎ 333-3456

Museum of Fine Arts ☎ 267-9300

Museum of Science ☎ 723-2500

New England Aquarium ☎ 973-5200

New England Conservatory
☎ 536-2412

Orpheum Theatre ☎ 482-0650

Sanders Theatre/Harvard
☎ 496-2222

Shubert Theatre ☎ 482-9393

Symphony Hall ☎ 266-1492

Ticketmaster ☎ 931-2000

Wang Center ☎ 482-9393

Wilbur Theatre ☎ 423-4008

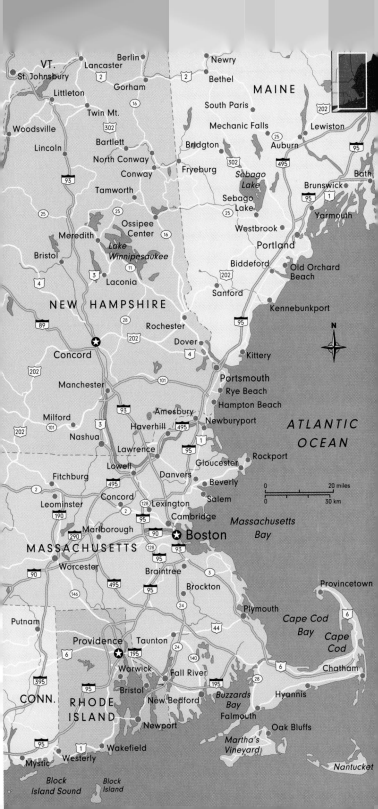

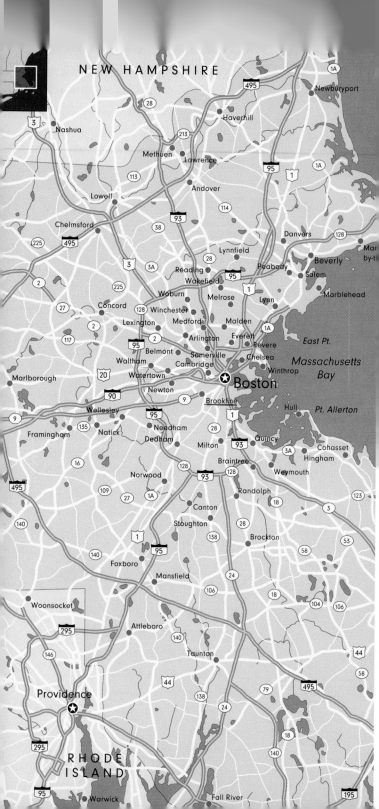

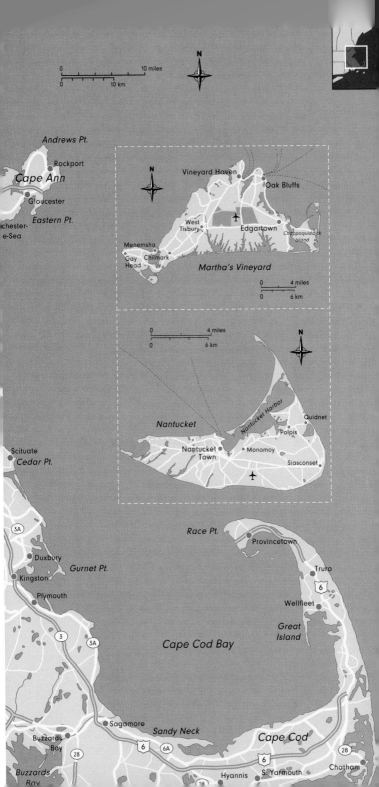

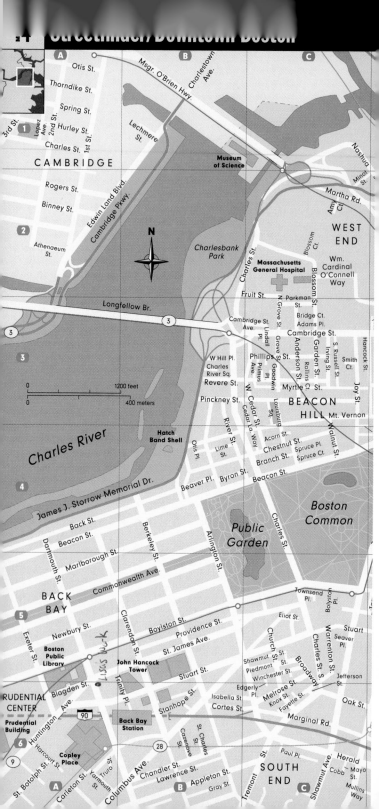

CAMBRIDGE

Otis St.
Thorndike St.
Spring St.
Hurley St.
Charles St.
3rd St.
Lopez Ave.
2nd St.
1st St.
Rogers St.
Binney St.
Atheneaum St.
Edwin Land Blvd.
Cambridge Pkwy.
Msgr. O'Brien Hwy.
Charlestown Ave.
Lechmere St.

Museum of Science

Nashua St.
Minot St.
Martha Rd.
Amy Ct.

WEST END

Charlesbank Park

Massachusetts General Hospital

Blossom Ct.
Wm. Cardinal O'Connell Way

Charles St.
Fruit St.
N Grove St.
Grove St.
Goodwin Pl.
Parkman St.
Bridge Ct.
Adams Pl.
Blossom St.
Garden St.
Irving St.
S. Russell St.
Hancock St.
Smith Ct.
Cambridge St.
Cambridge St. Ave.
Lindall Pl.
Anderson St.
Phillips St.
Primus Ave.
Rollins Pl.
W Hill Pl.
Charles River Sq.
Revere St.
Pinckney St.
Myrtle St.
Joy St.
Smith St.

N

Longfellow Br.
3

Cambridge St. Ave.

Louisburg Sq.
BEACON HILL
Mt. Vernon
W. Cedar St.
Cedar La. Way
Acorn St.
Chestnut St.
Branch St.
Spruce Pl.
Spruce Ct.
Walnut St.
Beacon St.

Charles River

Hatch Band Shell

Otis Pl.
River St.
Lime St.
Byron St.
Beaver Pl.

1200 feet
400 meters

Boston Common

James J. Storrow Memorial Dr.

Charles St.

Public Garden

Back St.
Beacon St.
Marlborough St.
Dartmouth St.
Berkeley St.
Arlington St.

Commonwealth Ave.

BACK BAY

Townsend Pl.
Boylston Pl.

Newbury St.
Exeter St.
Boylston St.
Clarendon St.
Providence St.
St. James Ave.
Eliot St.
Stuart St.
Seaver Pl.
Warrenton St.
Charles St. S.

Boston Public Library

John Hancock Tower

Stuart St.
Trinity Pl.
Church St.
Shawmut St.
Piedmont St.
Winchester St.
Broadway
Jefferson St.

Blagden St.

RUDENTIAL CENTER

90

Huntington Ave.
Stanhope St.
Edgerly Pl.
Isabella St.
Cortes St.
Knox St.
Fayette St.
Melrose St.
Oak St.

Marginal Rd.

Prudential Building

Back Bay Station

Copley Place

Harcourt St.
St. Botolph St.
Carleton St.
Yarmouth St.
Truro St.
28
Columbus Ave.
Chandler St.
Lawrence St.
St. Charles St.
Cazenove St.
Appleton St.
Gray St.
Tremont St.
Paul Pl.
Cobb
Shawmut Ave.

Herald St.
Mayo
Mullins Way

SOUTH END

9

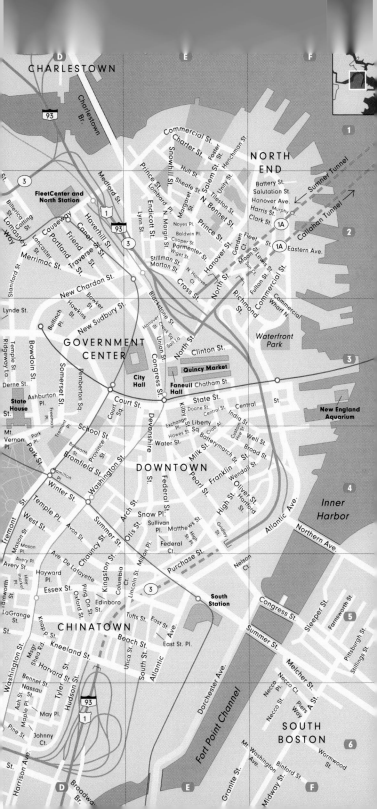

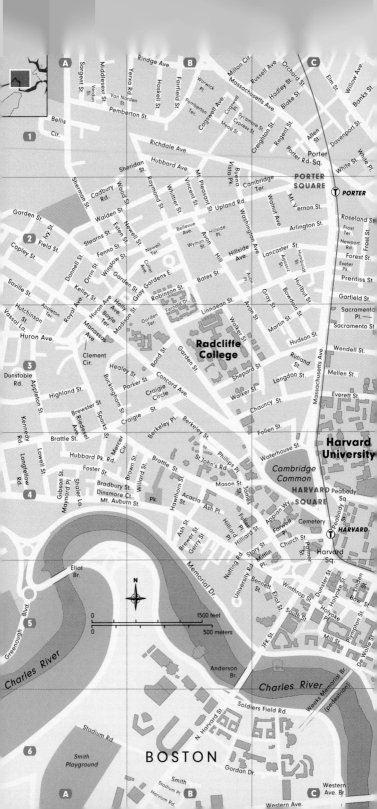

Letter codes refer to grid sectors on preceding map

Letter codes refer to grid sectors on preceding map

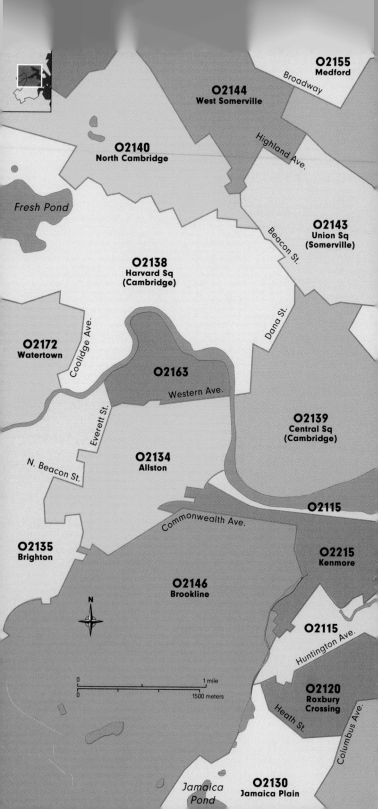

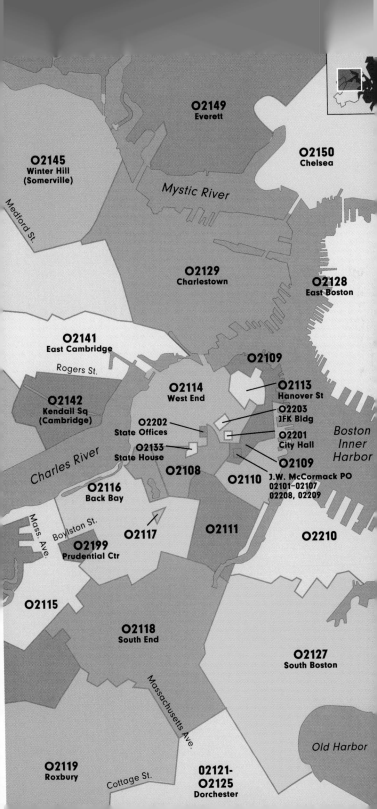

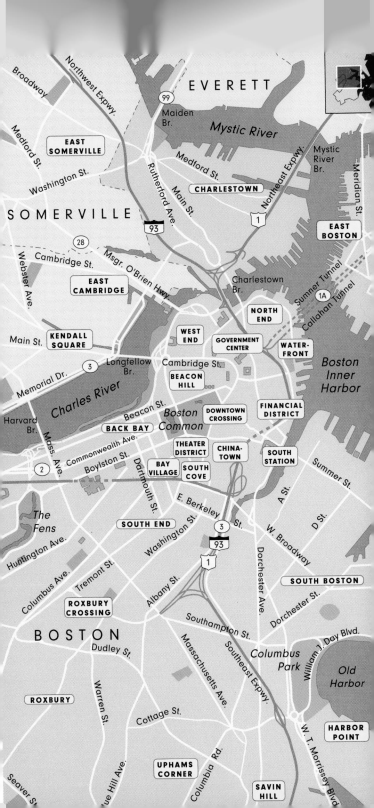

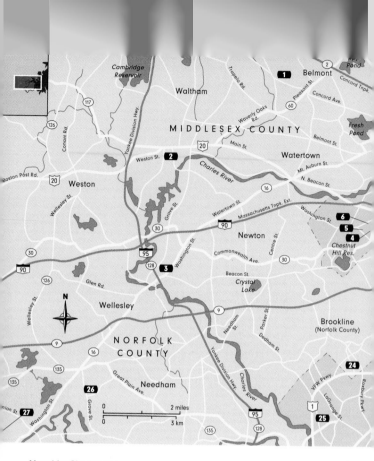

Listed by Site Number

Listed Alphabetically

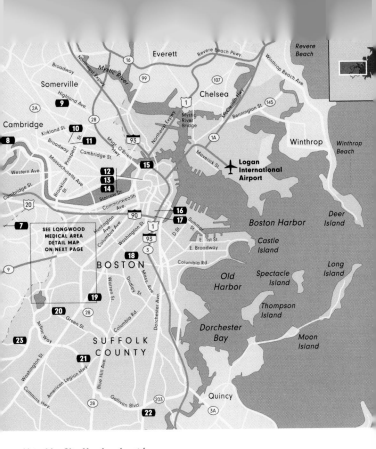

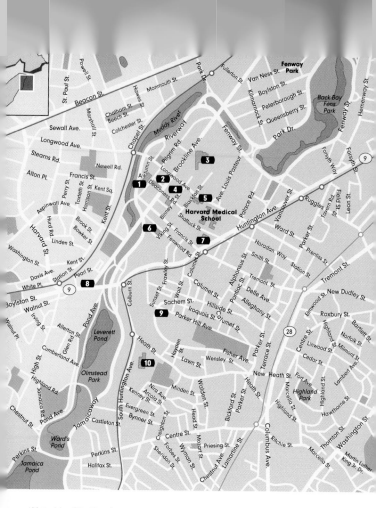

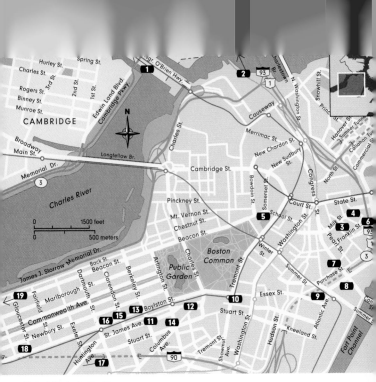

Listed Alphabetically

Australia, 12. 20 Park Plaza
☎ 248-8655

Austria, 5. 15 School St ☎ 227-3131

Belgium, 2. 300 Commercial St,
Malden ☎ 397-8566

Brazil, 12. 20 Park Plaza ☎ 542-4000

Canada, 17. 3 Copley Pl ☎ 262-3760

Cape Verde, 15. 535 Boylston St
☎ 353-0014

Chile, 4. 79 Milk St ☎ 426-1678

Colombia, 15. 535 Boylston St
☎ 536-6222

Denmark, 12. 20 Park Plaza
☎ 266-8418

Dominican Rep, 12. 20 Park Plaza
☎ 482-8121

France, 11. 31 St James Ave
☎ 542-7344

Germany, 17. 3 Copley Pl ☎ 536-4414

Great Britain, 8. 600 Atlantic Ave
☎ 248-9555

Greece, 19. 86 Beacon St
☎ 523-0100

Haiti, 16. 545 Boylston St ☎ 266-3660

Hungary, 1. 75 Cambridge Pkwy,
Cambridge ☎ 621-0886

Ireland, 15. 535 Boylston St
☎ 267-9330

Israel, 12. 20 Park Plaza ☎ 542-0041

Italy, 10. 100 Boylston St ☎ 542-0483

Japan, 8. 600 Atlantic Ave
☎ 973-9772

Mexico, 12. 20 Park Plaza
☎ 426-4942

Netherlands, 14. 6 St James Ave
☎ 542-8452

Norway, 7. 286 Congress St
☎ 423-2515

Peru, 15. 535 Boylston St ☎ 267-4050

Poland, 3. 31 Milk St ☎ 357-1980

Portugal, 18. 899 Boylston St
☎ 536-8740

Republic of Korea, 9.
One Financial Ctr ☎ 348-3660

Romania, 6. 85 E India Row
☎ 624-0228

Spain, 16. 545 Boylston St
☎ 536-2506

Sweden, 14. 286 Congress St
☎ 350-0111

Switzerland, 12. 20 Park Plaza
☎ 357-1617

Thailand, 13. 420 Boylston St
☎ 536-6552

Venezuela, 16. 545 Boylston St
☎ 266-9368

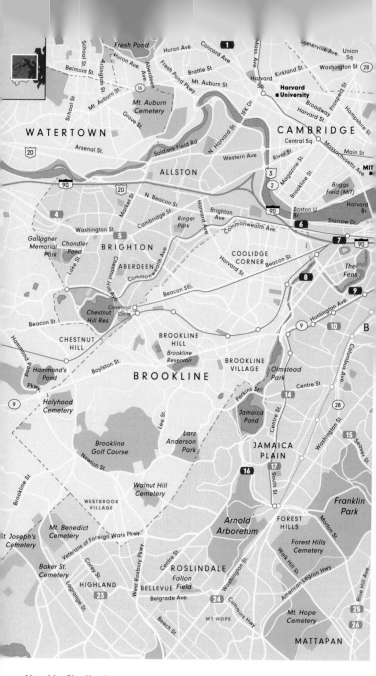

Listed Alphabetically

PUBLIC

Adams St, 29. 690 Adams St, Dorchester ☎ 436-6900

Boston Public, 45. 666 Boylston St ☎ 536-5400

Brighton, 5. 40 Academy Hill Rd, Brighton ☎ 782-6032

Charlestown, 30. 179 Main St, Charlestown ☎ 242-1248

Codman Sq, 27. 690 Washington St, Dorchester ☎ 436-8214

Connolly, 14. 433 Centre St, Jamaica Plain ☎ 522-1960

Dudley, 11. 65 Warren St, Roxbury ☎ 442-6186

East Boston, 2. 276 Meridian St, E Boston ☎ 569-0271

Egleston Sq, 15. 2044 Columbus Ave, Roxbury ☎ 445-4340

Faneuil, 4. 419 Faneuil St, Brighton ☎ 782-6705

Fields Corner, 22. 1520 Dorchester Ave, Dorchester ☎ 436-2155

Grove Hall, 18. 5 Crawford St, Dorchester ☎ 427-3337

Hyde Park, 26. 35 Harvard St, Hyde Park ☎ 361-2524

Jamaica Plain, 17. 12 Sedgwick St, Jamaica Plain ☎ 524-2053

Kirstein Business, 36. 20 City Hall Ave ☎ 523-0860

Lower Mills, 28. 27 Richmond St, Dorchester ☎ 298-7841

Mattapan, 25. 8 Hazelton St, Mattapan ☎ 298-9218

North End, 31. 25 Parmenter St ☎ 227-8135

Orient Heights, 3. 18 Barnes Ave, E Boston ☎ 567-2516

Parker Hill, 10. 1497 Tremont St, Roxbury ☎ 427-3820

Roslindale, 24. 4238 Washington St, Roslindale ☎ 323-2343

South Boston, 13. 646 E Broadway, S Boston ☎ 268-0180

Uphams Corner, 19. 500 Columbia Rd, Dorchester ☎ 265-0139

Washington Village, 12. 1226 Columbia Rd, S Boston ☎ 269-7239

West End, 32. 151 Cambridge St ☎ 523-3957

West Roxbury, 23. 1961 Centre St, W Roxbury ☎ 325-3147

PROFESSIONAL

Archives of American Art, 33. 87 Mt Vernon St ☎ 565-8444

Arnold Arboretum, 16. Arborway, Jamaica Plain ☎ 524-1718

Art Institute Boston, 7. 700 Beacon St ☎ 262-1223

Boston Architecture, 46. 320 Newbury St ☎ 536-9018

Boston Athenaeum, 35. 10½ Beacon St ☎ 227-0270

Boston Globe Newspaper, 20. 135 Morrissey Blvd ☎ 929-2000

Boston Herald Newspaper, 51. One Herald Sq ☎ 426-3000

Boston Psychoanalytic, 40. 15 Commonwealth Ave ☎ 266-0953

Bostonian Society, 37. 15 State St ☎ 720-3285

Charles River Associates, 44. 200 Clarendon St ☎ 266-0500

Christian Science Monitor, 48. 1 Norway St ☎ 450-2000

Congregational Library, 34. 14 Beacon St ☎ 523-0470

Crime & Justice Foundation, 41. 95 Berkeley St ☎ 426-9800

Federal Reserve Bank, 42. 600 Atlantic Ave ☎ 973-3397

Franklin Institute, 50. 41 Berkeley St ☎ 423-4630

French Library, 39. 53 Marlborough St ☎ 266-4351

Goethe Institute, 38. 170 Beacon St ☎ 262-6050

Kennedy Presidential, 21. Columbia Pt, Dorchester ☎ 929-4500

Mass Historical Society, 47. 1154 Boylston St ☎ 536-1608

Mass Horticultural Society, 49. 300 Mass Ave ☎ 536-9280

Museum of Fine Arts, 9. 465 Huntington Ave ☎ 267-9300

New Eng Historic Genealogic Society, 43. 101 Newbury St ☎ 536-5740

Smithsonian Astrophysical, 1. 60 Garden St, Cambridge ☎ 495-7461

Temple Israel, 8. 260 Riverway ☎ 566-3960

Zion Research, 6. 771 Commonwealth Ave ☎ 353-3724

MAP 12 Universities, Colleges & Schools

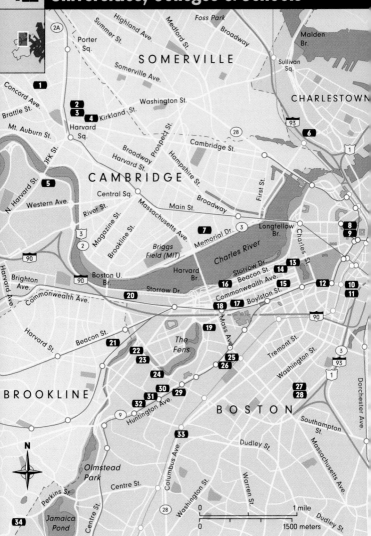

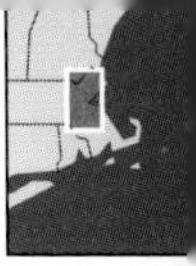

Listed by Site Number

1 University of Massachusetts–Lowell
2 Gordon College
3 Endicott College
4 Salem State College
5 Middlesex Community College
6 Tufts University
7 Bentley College
8 Brandeis University
9 Lasell College
10 Regis College
11 Tufts University School of Veterinary Medicine
12 Wellesley College
13 Babson College
14 Framingham State
15 Massachusetts Bay Community College
16 Mount Ida College
17 Pine Manor College
18 Boston College
19 University of Massachusetts-Boston
20 Laboure College
21 Eastern Nazarene College
22 Curry College
23 Stonehill College
24 Wheaton College

Listed Alphabetically

Babson College, 13.
Wellesley Ave, Wellesley
☎ 781/235-1200

Bentley College, 7.
175 Forest St, Waltham
☎ 781/891-2000

Boston College, 18.
140 Commonwealth Ave, Newton
☎ 552-8000

Brandeis University, 8.
415 South St, Waltham
☎ 781/736-2000

Curry College, 22.
1071 Blue Hill Ave, Milton
☎ 333-0500

Eastern Nazarene College, 21.
23 E Elm St, Quincy ☎ 773-6350

Endicott College, 3.
376 Hale St, Beverly
☎ 978/927-0585

Framinham State College, 14.
100 State St, Framingham
☎ 508/620-1220

Gordon College, 2.
255 Grapevine Rd, Wenham
☎ 978/927-2300

Laboure College, 20.
2120 Dorchester Ave
☎ 296-8300

Lasell College, 9.
1844 Commonwealth Ave, Newton
☎ 243-2000

Massachusetts Bay Community College, 15.
50 Oakland St, Wellesley
☎ 781/237-1100

Middlesex Community College, 5.
Springs Rd, Bedford
☎ 781/280-3200

Mount Ida College, 16.
777 Dedham St, Newton
☎ 969-7000

Pine Manor College, 17.
400 Heath St, Newton
☎ 731-7000

Regis College, 10.
235 Wellesley St, Weston
☎ 781/893-1820

Salem State College, 4.
352 Lafayette St, Salem
☎ 978/741-6000

Stonehill College, 23.
320 Washington Ave, Easton
☎ 508/565-1000

Tufts University, 6.
Packard Ave, Medford
☎ 781/628-5000

Tufts University School of Veterinary Medicine, 11.
Westboro Rd, North Grafton
☎ 508/839-5302

University of Massachusetts–Boston, 19.
Columbia Bay
☎ 287-5000

University of Massachusetts–Lowell, 1.
1 University Ave, Lowell
☎ 978/934-4000

Wellesley College, 12.
106 Central St, Wellesley
☎ 781/283-1000

Wheaton College, 24.
E Main St, Norton
☎ 508/285-7722

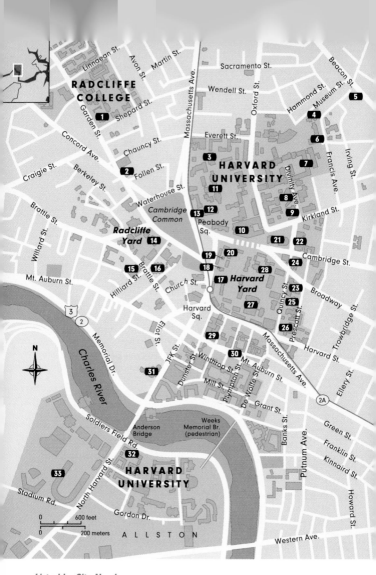

Listed by Site Number

1   Hilles Library
2   Longy Sch of Music
3   Harkness Commons & The Graduate Ctr
4   Rockefeller Hall
5   American Academy of Arts & Sciences
6   Divinity School
7   Harvard Biological Laboratories
8   Sherman Fairchild Biochemistry Lab
9   Adolphus Busch Hall
10 Science Center

11 Law School
12 Austin Hall
13 Hemenway Gym
14 Byerly Hall
15 Loeb Drama Center
16 Gutman Library
17 Massachusetts Hall
18 Harvard Hall
19 Holden Chapel
20 Stoughton Hall
21 Memorial Hall/ Sanders Theater
22 George Gund Hall
23 Fogg Museum

24 Arthur M Sackler Museum
25 Carpenter Center for the Visual Arts
26 Harvard Union
27 Widener Library
28 Memorial Church
29 Holyoke Center
30 Harvard Lampoon Castle
31 Kennedy School of Government
32 Harvard Business School
33 Soldiers Field

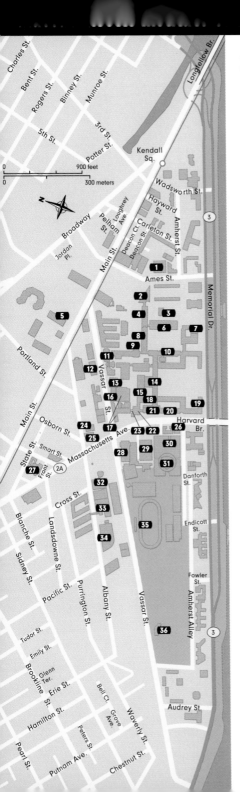

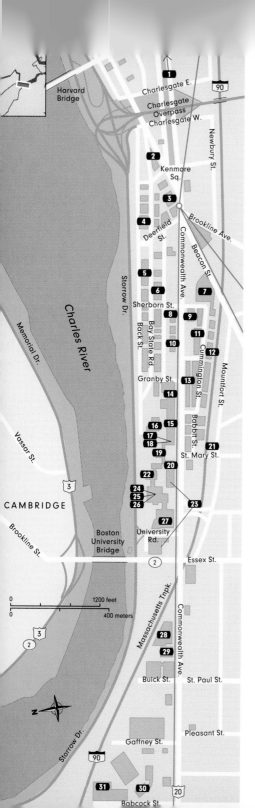

Airline	Terminal	A	B	C	D	E
Aer Lingus ☎ 800/223-6537						●
Air Alliance ☎ 800/776-3000						●
Air Atlantic/Canadian Airlines ☎ 800/426-7000						●
Alitalia ☎ 800/223-5730	(Departures Only)				●	●
	(Int'l Arrivals Only)					●
American ☎ 800/433-7300			●	●		
	(Int'l Arrivals Only)					●
American Eagle ☎ 800/433-7300			●			
America West ☎ 800/235-9292			●			
ATA ☎ 800/225-2995						●
British Airways ☎ 800/247-9297						●
Business Express/Delta Connection ☎ 800/345-3400				●		
Cape Air ☎ 800/352-0714		●				
Canadian Airlines ☎ 800/426-7000						●
Charter Flights (most)					●	
Colgan Air ☎ 800/272-5488		●				
Comair ☎ 800/354-9822				●		
Continental ☎ 800/525-0280		●				
Delta Airlines/Delta Express ☎ 800/221-1212			●			
Delta Shuttle ☎ 800/221-1212	(LaGuardia only)		●			
Eastwind Airlines ☎ 800/644-3592		●				
Icelandair ☎ 800/223-5500						●
KLM ☎ 800/374-7747						●
Korean Air ☎ 800/438-5000						●
Lufthansa ☎ 800/645-3880						●
Midway Airlines ☎ 800/446-4392			●			
Midwest Express ☎ 800/452-2022		●				
Northwest Airlines ☎ 800/225-2525						●
Olympic ☎ 800/223-1226						●
Qantas ☎ 800/227-4500						●
Sabena ☎ 800/955-2000	(Departures Only)			●		
	(Int'l Arrivals Only)					●
Spirit Airlines ☎ 800/772-7117		●				
Swissair ☎ 800/221-4750						●
TAP Air Portugal ☎ 800/221-7370						●
TWA/TW Express ☎ 800/221-2000				●		
United/United Express ☎ 800/241-6522				●		
US Airways/US Airways Express ☎ 800/428-4322			●			
	(Int'l Arrivals Only)					●
US Airways Shuttle ☎ 800/428-4322	(LaGuardia Only)	●				
Valujet ☎ 800/825-8538					●	
Virgin Atlantic ☎ 800/862-8621	(Int'l Arrivals Only)					●

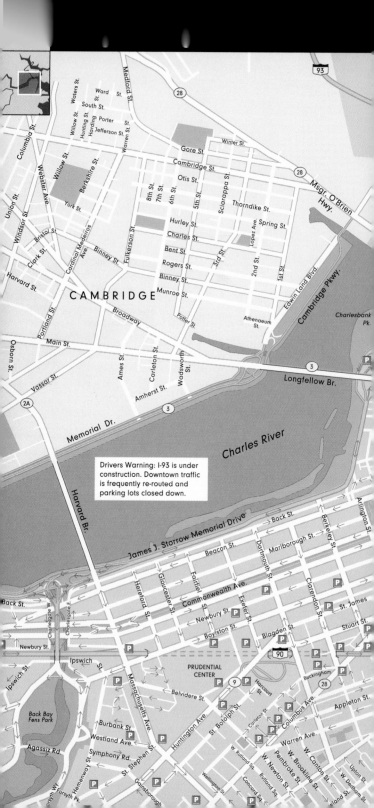

Drivers Warning: I-93 is under construction. Downtown traffic is frequently re-routed and parking lots closed down.

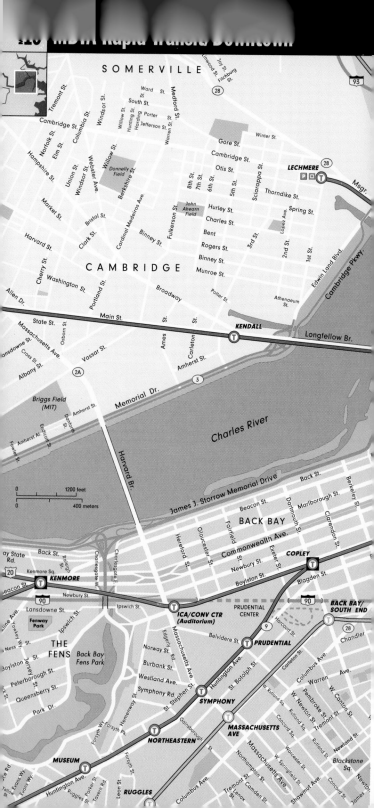

SOMERVILLE

93

CAMBRIDGE

Tremont St.

Cambridge St.

Norfolk St.

Elm St.

Hampshire St.

Union St.

Webster Ave.

Windsor St.

Columbia St.

Windsor St.

Willow St.

Ward St.

South St.

Hunting St.

Harding St.

Porter St.

Jefferson St.

Warren St.

Medford St.

Fitchburg St.

Linwood St.

Joy St.

28

Winter St.

Gore St.

Cambridge St.

Otis St.

Sciarappa St.

Thorndike St.

LECHMERE

28

Msgr.

Donnelly Field

Bertshire St.

Cardinal Medeiros Ave.

Binney St.

Fulkerson St.

8th St.

7th St.

6th St.

5th St.

John Ahearn Field

Hurley St.

Charles St.

Bent

Rogers St.

Binney St.

3rd St.

2nd St.

1st St.

Lopez Ave.

Spring St.

Edwin Land Blvd.

Cambridge Pkwy.

Market St.

Harvard St.

Clark St.

Bristol St.

Portland St.

Broadway

Munroe St.

Potter St.

Athenaeum St.

Cherry St.

Washington St.

Allen Dr.

Main St.

State St.

Osborn St.

KENDALL

Longfellow Br.

Massachusetts Ave.

Lansdowne St.

Cross St.

Albany St.

Vassar St.

2A

Ames St.

Carleton St.

Amherst St.

3

Briggs Field (MIT)

Memorial Dr.

Amherst St.

Amherst Al.

Endicott St.

Danforth St.

Fowler St.

Charles River

Harvard Br.

0   1200 feet
0   400 meters

James J. Storrow Memorial Drive

Back St.

Beacon St.

Berkeley St.

Dartmouth St.

Marlborough St.

Clarendon St.

BACK BAY

Fairfield St.

Hereford St.

Gloucester St.

Commonwealth Ave.

Exeter St.

COPLEY

ay State Rd.

Back St.

Raleigh St.

Charlesgate W.

Charlesgate E.

Newbury St.

Boylston St.

Blagden St.

20

Kenmore Sq.

KENMORE

90

Newbury St.

Ipswich St.

90

BACK BAY/ SOUTH END

Beacon St.

Lansdowne St.

ICA/CONV CTR (Auditorium)

PRUDENTIAL CENTER

Harcourt St.

28

Chandler

Fenway Park

Ipswich St.

Edgerly Rd.

Massachusetts Ave.

Belvidere St.

9

PRUDENTIAL

Clearway St.

Columbus Ave.

Warren Ave.

THE FENS

Back Bay Fens Park

Boylston St.

Jersey St.

Kilmarnock St.

Van Ness St.

Norway St.

Burbank St.

Westland Ave.

St. Botolph St.

W. Newton St.

W. Rutland Sq.

Pembroke St.

W. Canton St.

Tremont St.

Peterborough St.

Queensberry St.

Park Dr.

Symphony Rd.

Hemenway St.

Stephen St.

Huntington Ave.

SYMPHONY

Concord St.

W. Springfield St.

Rutland St.

Newland St.

Blackstone Sq.

Forsyth Pk.

Forsyth Wy.

Gainsborough St.

MASSACHUSETTS AVE

Massachusetts Ave.

Northampton St.

Camden St.

Lenox St.

Shawmut Ave.

Concord St.

NORTHEASTERN

MUSEUM

Huntington Ave.

Forsyth St.

Evans Wy.

Evans Wy.

Leon St.

Ruggles St.

Parker St.

Tavern Rd.

RUGGLES

Columbus Ave.

Tremont St.

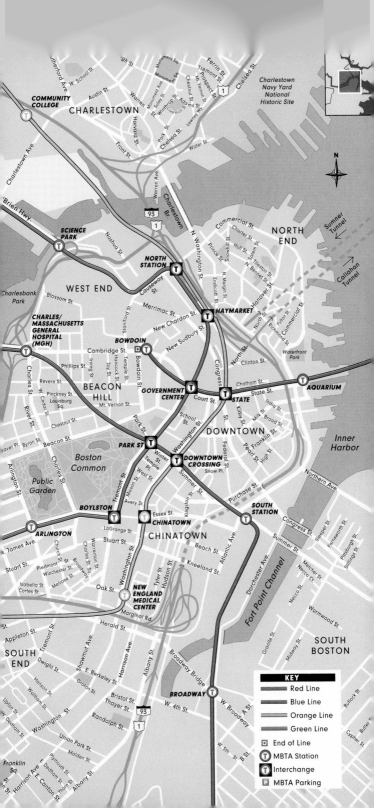

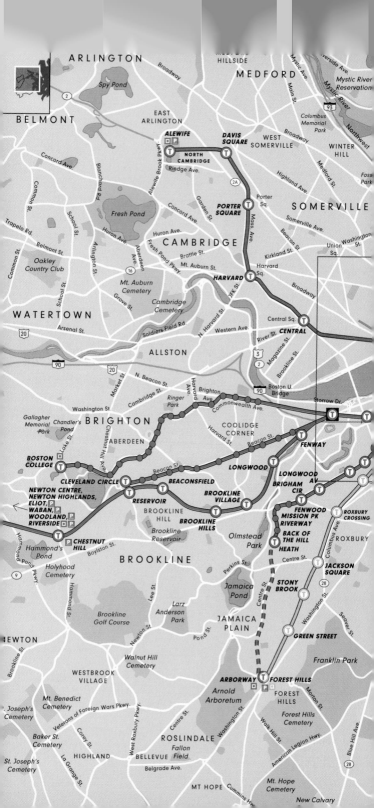

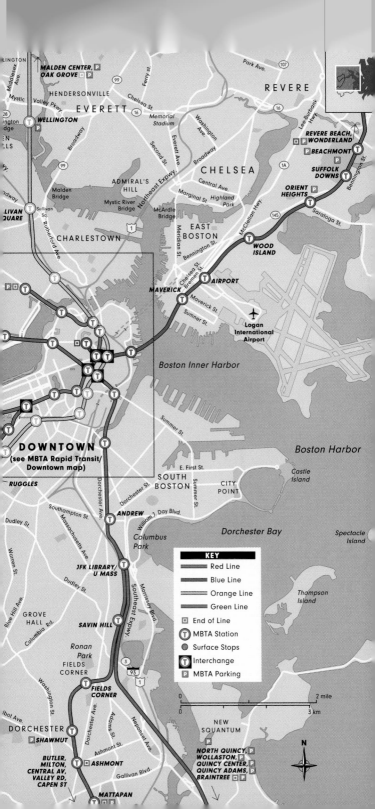

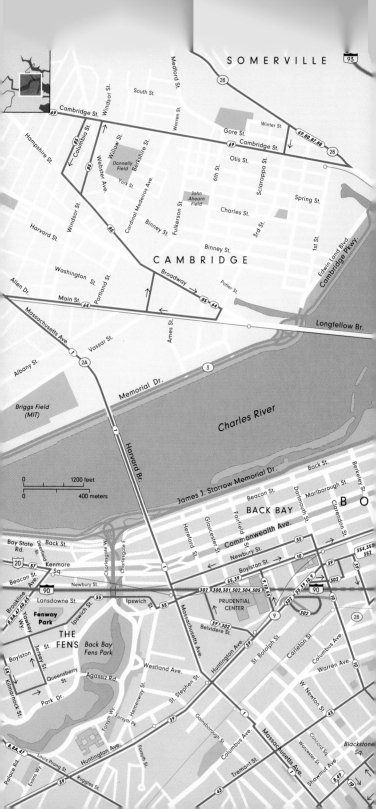

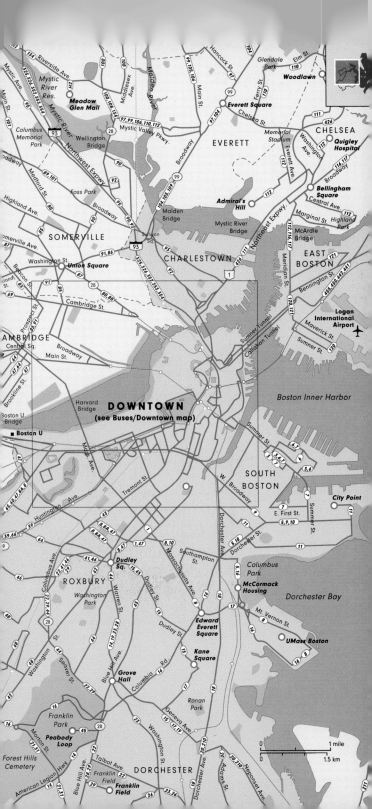

MAP 23 Commuter Rail Lines & Outer Ⓣ Stops

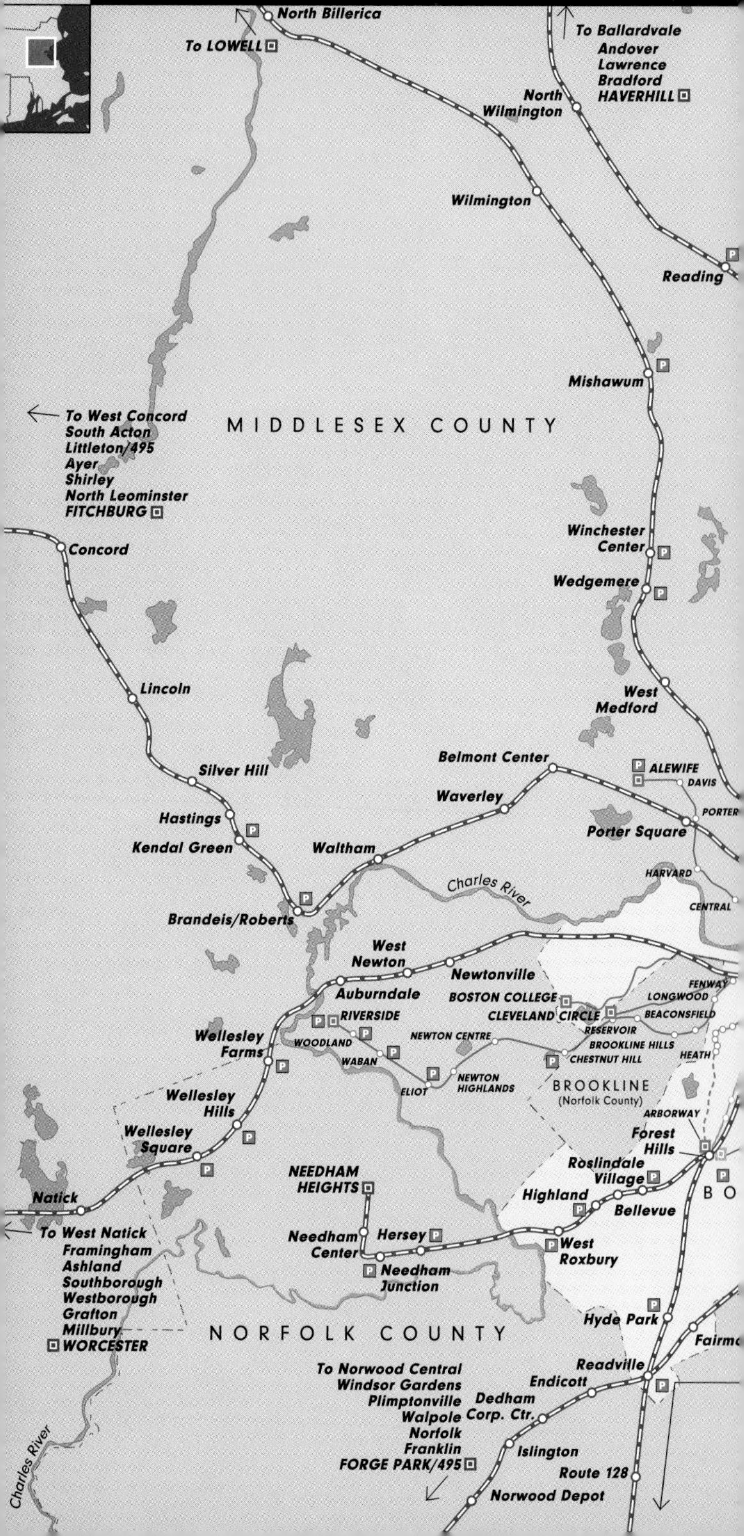
North Billerica
To LOWELL
To Ballardvale
Andover
Lawrence
Bradford
HAVERHILL
North Wilmington
Wilmington
Reading
Mishawum
MIDDLESEX COUNTY
To West Concord
South Acton
Littleton/495
Ayer
Shirley
North Leominster
FITCHBURG
Concord
Winchester Center
Wedgemere
Lincoln
West Medford
Belmont Center
ALEWIFE
DAVIS
Silver Hill
Waverley
PORTER
Hastings
Porter Square
Kendal Green
Waltham
HARVARD
Charles River
CENTRAL
Brandeis/Roberts
West Newton
Newtonville
Auburndale
FENWAY
BOSTON COLLEGE
LONGWOOD
RIVERSIDE
CLEVELAND CIRCLE
BEACONSFIELD
Wellesley Farms
WOODLAND
NEWTON CENTRE
RESERVOIR
BROOKLINE HILLS
WABAN
CHESTNUT HILL
HEATH
NEWTON HIGHLANDS
ELIOT
BROOKLINE
(Norfolk County)
Wellesley Hills
ARBORWAY
Forest Hills
Wellesley Square
NEEDHAM HEIGHTS
Roslindale Village
Natick
Highland
Bellevue
BO
To West Natick
Framingham
Ashland
Southborough
Westborough
Grafton
Millbury
WORCESTER
Needham Center
Hersey
West Roxbury
Needham Junction
Hyde Park
NORFOLK COUNTY
Fairm
Readville
To Norwood Central
Windsor Gardens
Plimptonville
Walpole
Norfolk
Franklin
FORGE PARK/495
Endicott
Dedham Corp. Ctr.
Islington
Route 128
Norwood Depot
Charles River

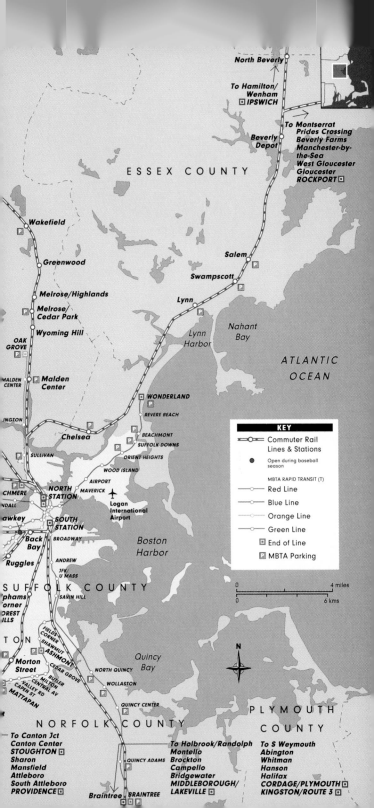

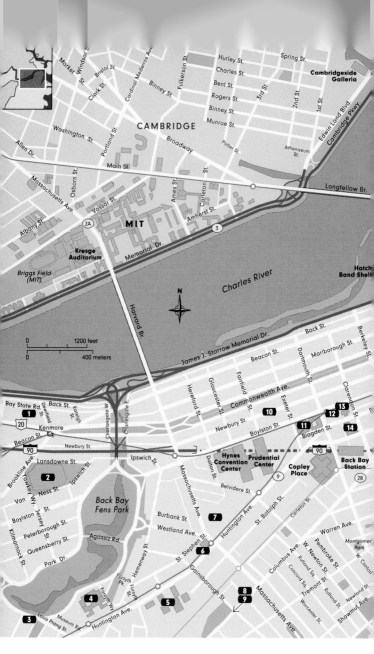

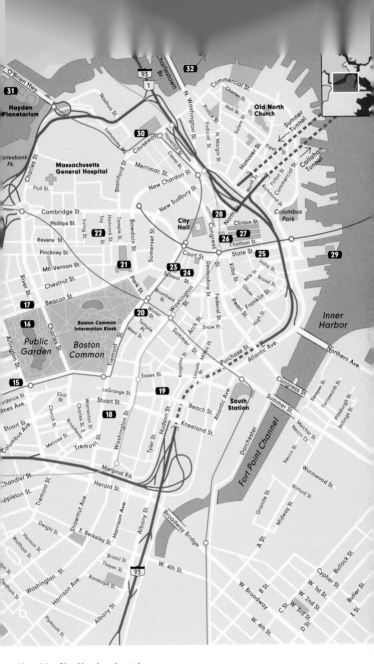

MAP 25 Freedom Trail & Black Heritage Trail

99

Main St.

School St.

Elm St.

High St.

Green St.

Cross St.

Cedar St.

Monument Sq.

Lexington St.

Tremont St.

Ferrin St.

Decatur St.

Chelsea St.

16

Rutherford Ave.

Austin St.

Warren St.

Cordis St.

Pleasant St.

Mt. Vernon St.

Chestnut St.

Lowney Wy.

1

Charlestown Navy Yard
National Historic Site

Washington St.

Lynde St.

Union St.

Main St.

Harvard St.

Monument Ave.

Huron St.

Soley St.

Winthrop St.

Adams St.

Park St.

CHARLESTOWN

Front St.

Chelsea St.

Water St.

Wapping St.

15

USS
Constitution

CAMBRIDGE

Charlestown Ave.

Charlestown Br.

93

1

N. Washington St.

Commercial St.

Charter St.

Snowhill St.

Hull St.

14

13

Salem St.

N. Bennet St.

Fleet St.

Hanover Ave.

Harris St.

Clark St.

Msgr. O'Brien Hwy.

Museum
of Science

Hayden
Planetarium

Nashua St.

Lomasney Wy.

North Station/
FleetCenter

Causeway St.

Haverhill St.

Friend St.

Canal St.

Prince St.

N. Margin St.

Endicott St.

Hanover St.

North St.

12

Commercial St.

Charlesbank
Park

Charles St.

Fruit St.

Blossom St.

N. Grove St.

Parkman St.

Stanford St.

Merrimac St.

New Chardon St.

New Sudbury St.

Cross St.

Hanover St.

Creek St.

Cambridge St.

Phillips St.

7

6

5

Smith Ct.

Temple St.

Bowdoin St.

City Hall

Congress St.

11

Quincy
Market

Chatham St.

Revere St.

4

3

Hancock St.

BEACON
HILL

Somerset St.

Court St.

10

State St.

Pinckney St.

10

2

Derne St.

9

State
House

School St.

9

7

India St.

Broad St.

8

Mt. Vernon St.

Cedar St.

Louisburg Sq.

Vernon St.

Walnut St.

2

5

4

8

Devonshire St.

Kilby St.

Milk St.

Oliver St.

Chestnut St.

Branch St.

River St.

Byron St.

1

Beacon St.

Park St.

Bromfield St.

Washington St.

Federal St.

Arch St.

Pearl St.

Franklin St.

High St.

Public
Garden

Charles St.

Boston
Common

1

Winter St.

Temple Pl.

West St.

Summer St.

Otis St.

Snow Pl.

Purchase St.

Atlantic Ave.

Congress St.

Arlington St.

Providence St.

James Ave.

Stuart St.

Eliot St.

Stuart St.

Charles St. S.

Church St.

Broadway

Tremont St.

Oak St.

Washington St.

Essex St.

LaGrange St.

Beach St.

Kingston St.

Kneeland St.

Tyler St.

Hudson St.

South
Station

Summer St.

Isabella St.

Cortes St.

Chandler St.

90

Marginal Rd.

1

93

Appleton St.

Herald St.

Harrison Ave.

Albany St.

Broadway

E. Berkeley St.

Shawmut Ave.

KEY

········ Freedom Trail
(red line on sidewalk)

- - - Freedom Trail
(Bunker Hill extension)

●●●● Black Heritage
Trail

MAP 25

MAP 26 Architecture

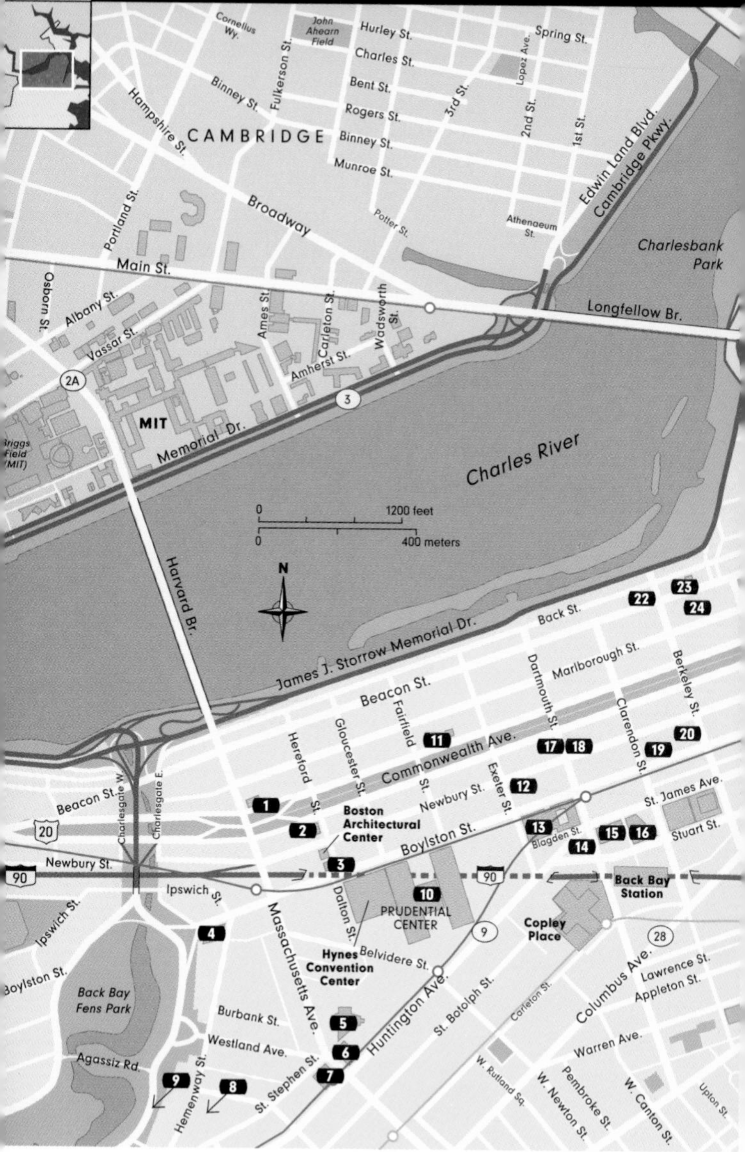
Cornelius Wy.
John Ahearn Field
Hurley St.
Spring St.
Charles St.
Lopez Ave.
Fulkerson St.
Binney St.
Bent St.
3rd St.
Rogers St.
2nd St.
1st St.
Hampshire St.
CAMBRIDGE
Binney St.
Munroe St.
Edwin Land Blvd.
Cambridge Pkwy.
Portland St.
Broadway
Potter St.
Athenaeum St.
Charlesbank Park
Main St.
Osborn St.
Albany St.
Ames St.
Carleton St.
Wadsworth St.
Longfellow Br.
Vassar St.
Amherst St.
2A
3
MIT
Briggs Field (MIT)
Memorial Dr.
Charles River
0
1200 feet
0
400 meters
N
Harvard Br.
Back St.
James J. Storrow Memorial Dr.
Marlborough St.
Dartmouth St.
Berkeley St.
Beacon St.
Fairfield St.
Gloucester St.
Hereford St.
Clarendon St.
Commonwealth Ave.
Exeter St.
Newbury St.
Beacon St.
Charlesgate W.
Charlesgate E.
20
Boston Architectural Center
Boylston St.
St. James Ave.
Stuart St.
Blagden St.
Newbury St.
90
Ipswich St.
Dalton St.
PRUDENTIAL CENTER
90
Back Bay Station
Copley Place
9
28
Ipswich St.
Massachusetts Ave.
Hynes Convention Center
Belvidere St.
Boylston St.
Back Bay Fens Park
Huntington Ave.
St. Botolph St.
Carleton St.
Columbus Ave.
Lawrence St.
Appleton St.
Burbank St.
Westland Ave.
Warren Ave.
Agassiz Rd.
Hemenway St.
St. Stephen St.
W. Rutland Sq.
W. Newton St.
Pembroke St.
W. Canton St.
Upton St.
1
2
3
4
5
6
7
8
9
10
11
12
13
14
15
16
17
18
19
20
22
23
24

Listed by Site Number

1 Ames Mansion
2 Burrage Mansion
3 Institute of Contemporary Art
4 Mass Historical Soc
5 Christian Science Ctr
6 Horticultural Hall
7 Symphony Hall
8 Museum of Fine Arts
9 Gardner Museum
10 Prudential Center
11 Algonquin Club
12 Exeter St Theatre
13 Boston Public Library
14 Copley Place
15 Copley Plaza Hotel
16 Hancock Tower
17 Hotel Vendome
18 270 Dartmouth St
19 The New England
20 Louis Boston
21 Cyclorama
22 Emerson College
23 Fisher Junior College
24 Gibson House
25 Baylies Mansion
26 Colonial Theatre
27 Kennedy Library
28 Dorchester Heights Memorial

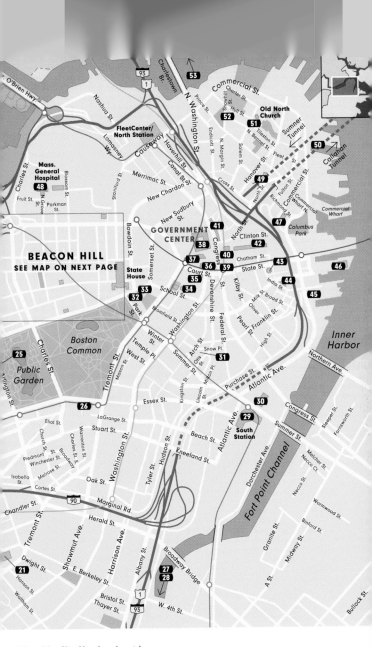

Listed by Site Number

Listed Alphabetically

Acorn St, 63.

Algonquin Club, 11.
217 Commonwealth Ave

Ames Mansion, 1.
355 Commonwealth Ave

Appleton Mansions, 68.
39–40 Beacon St

Baylies Mansion, 25.
5 Commonwealth Ave

Blackstone Block, 41. Haymarket Sq

Boston Athenaeum, 33.
10½ Beacon St

Boston Public Library, 13.
666 Boylston St

Bunker Hill Monument, 53.
Monument Square

Burrage Mansion, 2.
314 Commonwealth Ave

Charles St, 54.

Chestnut St, 64.

Christian Science Center, 5.
175 Huntington Ave

City Hall, 38. I City Hall Square

Clough House, 51. 21 Unity St

Colonial Theatre, 26. 106 Boylston St

Copley Place, 14. I Copley Place

Copley Plaza Hotel, 15. Copley Sq

Custom House, 43. State & India Sts

Cyclorama, 21. 539 Tremont St

Dorchester Heights Memorial, 28.
Thomas Park/6th St, Dorchester

89–93 Franklin St, 31.

Emerson College, 22. 7 Arlington St

Exeter St Theatre, 12. 26 Exeter St

Faneuil Hall, 39. Faneuil Hall
Marketplace

Federal Reserve Bank, 30.
600 Atlantic Ave

5 Pinckney St, 57.

Fisher Junior College, 23. 118 Beacon St

Fleet Bank, 36. 28 State St

Flour & Grain Exchange, 44. 177 Milk St

43 S Russell St, 56.

44 Hull St, 52.

Gibson House, 24. 137 Beacon St

Hancock Tower, 16. Copley Square

Harbor Towers, 45. 85 E India Row

Harding House, 32. 16 Beacon St

Harrison Gray Otis House #1, 55. 141 Cambridge St

Harrison Gray Otis House #2, 61. 85 Mt Vernon St

Harrison Gray Otis House #3, 66.
45 Beacon St

Horticultural Hall, 6. 300 Mass Ave

Hotel Vendome, 17.
160 Commonwealth Ave

Institute of Contemporary Art, 3.
955 Boylston St

Isabella Stewart Gardner Museum, 9. 280 Fenway

Kennedy Library, 27.
Columbia Pt, Dorchester

Louis Boston, 20. 234 Berkeley St

Louisburg Square, 62. Mt Vernon St

Mass General Hospital, 48. 55 Fruit St

Mass Historical Society, 4.
1154 Boylston St

Mass State House, 58. Beacon St

Mercantile Wharf, 47.
Atlantic Ave & Richmond St

Museum of Fine Arts, 8.
465 Huntington Ave

New England Aquarium, 46.
250 Atlantic Ave

Old City Hall, 34. 45 School St

Old Statehouse, 35. 206 Washington St

Pierce-Hichborn House, 49.
29 North Square

Prudential Center, 10. 800 Boylston St

Quincy Market, 42. Faneuil Hall
Marketplace

Sears Crescent, 37.
Government Center

17 Chestnut St, 59.

70–75 Beacon St, 65.

60 State St, 40.

Somerset Club, 67. 42 Beacon St

South Station, 29.
Summer St & Atlantic Ave

Symphony Hall, 7. 301 Mass Ave

The New England, 19. 501 Boylston St

34 Beacon St, 69.

29A Chestnut St, 60.

270 Dartmouth St, 18.

Union Wharf, 50. 323 Commercial St

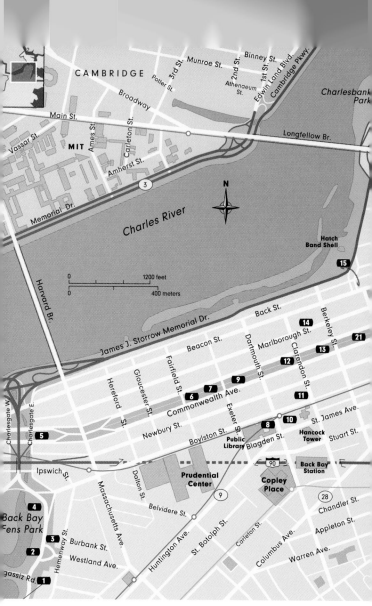

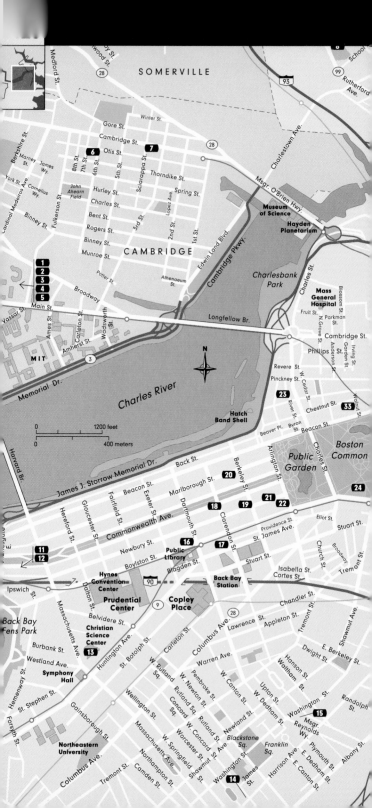

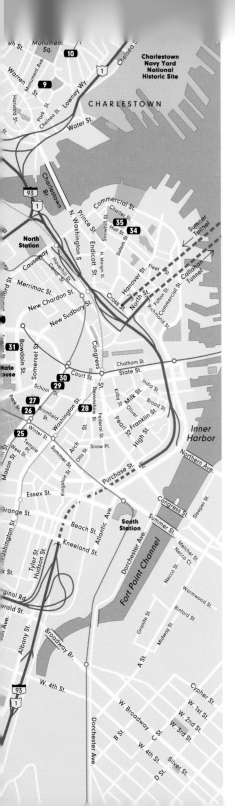

Listed Alphabetically

CHURCHES

Arlington St Church, 22.
351 Boylston St ☎ 536-7050.
Unitarian-Universalist.

Cathedral of the Holy Cross, 15.
1400 Washington St
☎ 542-5682. Catholic.

Christ Church, 1. Garden St,
Cambridge ☎ 876-0200. Episcopal.

Christ Church (Old North), 34.
193 Salem St ☎ 523-6676. Episcopal.

**Christian Science Mother
Church, 13.** 175 Huntington Ave
☎ 450-2000.

Church of the Advent, 23.
30 Brimmer St ☎ 523-2377. Episcopal.

Church of the Covenant, 19.
67 Newbury St ☎ 266-7480.
Presbyterian.

**Church of the Immaculate
Conception, 14.** 775 Harrison St
☎ 536-8440. Catholic.

Emmanuel Episcopal, 21.
15 Newbury St ☎ 536-3355.

First Baptist Church of Boston, 18.
110 Commonwealth Ave ☎ 267-3148.

**First and Second Church of
Boston, 20.** 66 Marlborough St
☎ 267-6730. Unitarian-Universalist.

First Church Congregational, 3.
11 Garden St, Cambridge ☎ 876-5829.

First Parish Church, 2. 3 Church St,
Cambridge ☎ 876-7772.
Unitarian-Universalist.

King's Chapel, 29. 58 Tremont St
☎ 523-1749. Unitarian-Universalist.

Old South Church, 16.
645 Boylston St
☎ 536-1970. Church of Christ.

Old South Meeting House, 28.
294 Washington St ☎ 482-6439

Old West Church, 32.
131 Cambridge St
☎ 227-5088. Methodist.

Park St Church, 26. 1 Park St
☎ 523-3383. Congregational.

Sacred Heart Church, 6. 49 Sixth St,
Cambridge ☎ 547-0399. Catholic.

St Francis de Sales, 10.
303 Bunker Hill, Charlestown
☎ 242-0147. Catholic.

St Francis of Assisi, 7.
42 Sciarappa St, Cambridge
☎ 876-6754. Catholic.

St John Evangelist, 31.
35 Bowdoin St ☎ 227-5242. Episcopal.

St Mary's, 9. 46 Winthrop St,
Charlestown ☎ 242-2196. Catholic.

St Paul's Cathedral, 25.
138 Tremont St ☎ 482-5800.
Episcopal.

Society of Friends, 33. 6 Chestnut St
☎ 227-9118. Quaker.

Temple Israel, 12. 260 Riverway
☎ 566-3960. Jewish.

Trinity Church, 17. Copley Square
☎ 536-0944. Episcopal.

CEMETERIES

Central Burying Ground, 24.
Tremont St/Boston Common

Copp's Hill Burying Ground, 35.
Charter St

Granary Burying Ground, 27. Park &
Tremont Sts

King's Chapel Burying Ground, 30.
58 Tremont St

Mt Auburn Cemetery, 4.
Mt Auburn St, Cambridge

**Old Burying Ground (First Parish
Church), 5.** Garden St, Cambridge

Phipps St Burying Ground, 8.
Phipps St, Charlestown

Walter St Burying Ground, 11.
Arnold Arboretum, Roslindale

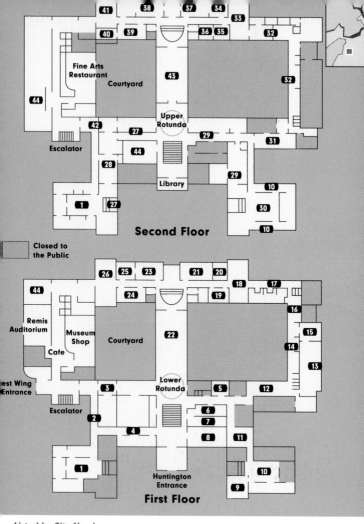

Second Floor

- 41
- 38
- 37
- 34
- 33
- 40
- 39
- 36
- 35
- 32
- Fine Arts Restaurant
- 43
- Courtyard
- 32
- 44
- 32
- Upper Rotunda
- 42
- 27
- 29
- 31
- Escalator
- 44
- 28
- 29
- 29
- Library
- 10
- 1
- 27
- 30
- 10

First Floor

- 26
- 25
- 23
- 21
- 20
- 18
- 17
- 44
- 24
- 19
- 16
- Remis Auditorium
- Museum Shop
- Courtyard
- 22
- 15
- Cafe
- 14
- West Wing Entrance
- 13
- 3
- 5
- 12
- Escalator
- 2
- 6
- 4
- 7
- Lower Rotunda
- 8
- 11
- 1
- 10
- Huntington Entrance
- 9

Closed to the Public

Listed by Site Number

1 Japanese Art	**16** 19th-C American	**30** Roman Art
2 Islamic Art	**17** American Federal	**31** Medieval Art
3 Brown Gallery	**18** Copley & Contemp	**32** Euro Decorative Arts
4 Indian Art	**19** American Neo-Classic & Romantic	**33** Impressionism
5 Egyptian Mummies	**20** Amer Folk Painting	**34** 19th-C French & Eng
6 Graphics	**21** 19th-C Landscape	**35** Post-Impressionism
7 Musical Instruments	**22** American Modern	**36** Coolidge Collection
8 Nubian Art	**23** American Masters	**37** 18th-C Italian
9 Etruscan Art	**24** Early 20th-C Amer	**38** Dutch & Flemish Art
10 Greek Art	**25** Amer Impressionism	**39** Renaissance
11 Near-Eastern Art	**26** 20th-C Amer & Euro	**40** Spanish Chapel
12 18th-C Amer Furniture	**27** Chinese Art	**41** Baroque Art
13 18th-C French Art	**28** Bernat Galleries	**42** Himalayan Art
14 18th-C Boston	**29** Egyptian Art	**43** Tapestries
15 English Silver		**44** Special Exhibitions

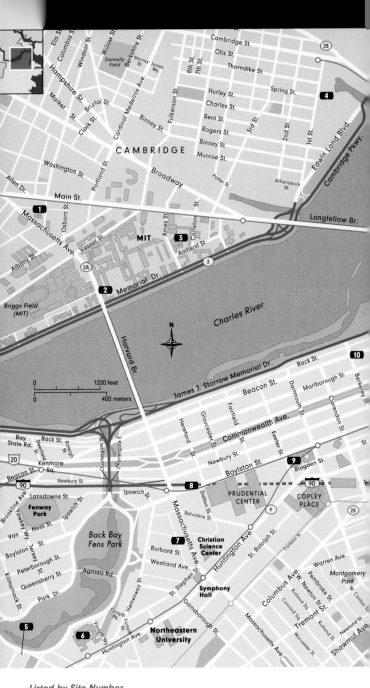

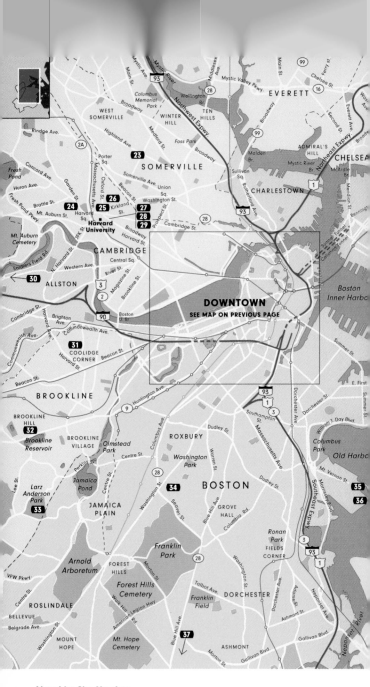

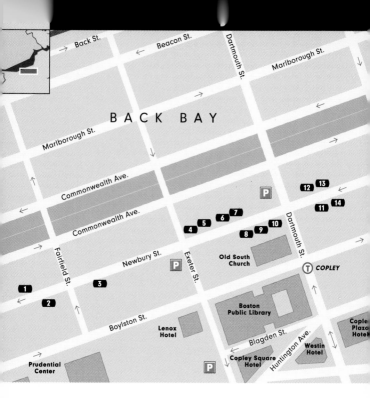

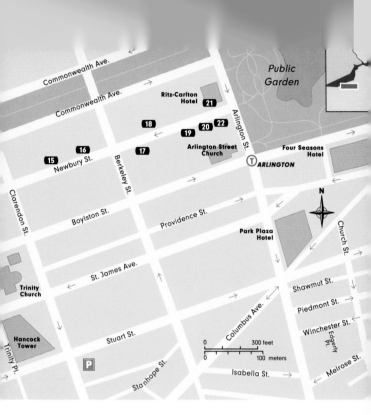

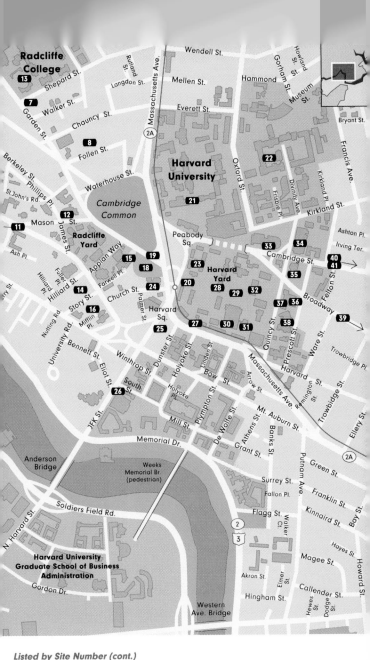

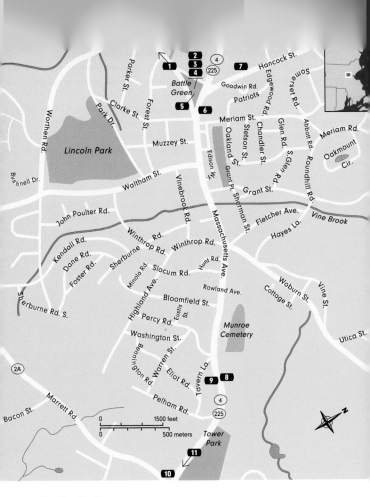

Listed by Site Number

1. Paul Revere Capture Site
2. Battle Green
3. Line of Battle Boulder
4. Revolutionary Monument
5. Minuteman Statue
6. Buckman Tavern
7. Hancock-Clarke House
8. Percy's Reinforcement Site
9. Munroe Tavern
10. Museum of our National Heritage
11. Old Schwamb Mill

Listed Alphabetically

Battle Green, 2. 1875 Mass Ave

Buckman Tavern, 6. 1 Bedford St
☎ 781/862-5598

Hancock-Clarke House, 7.
35 Hancock St ☎ 781/861-0928

Line of Battle Boulder, 3.
Battle Green

Minuteman Statue, 5.
Battle Green

Munroe Tavern, 9. 1332 Mass Ave
☎ 781/674-9238

**Museum of Our National
Heritage, 10.** 33 Marrett Rd
☎ 781/861-6559

Old Schwamb Mill, 11.
17 Mill Lane, Arlington ☎ 781/643-0554

Paul Revere Capture Site, 1.
Lexington Rd, Lincoln

Percy's Reinforcement Site, 8.
Mass Ave opposite Munroe Tavern

Revolutionary Monument, 4.
Battle Green

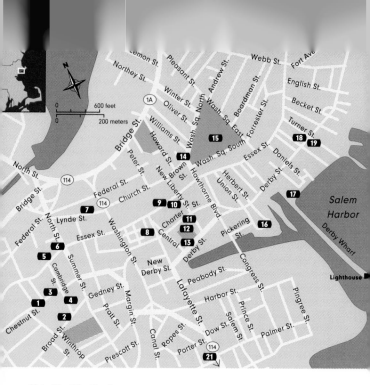

Listed on map:
1 TO IPSWICH & NEWBURYPORT
133 Essex
22
Essex River
Essex Bay
Wingaershe
Concord St.
West Gloucester
YMCA Camp
Atlantic
133
Concord St.
128
Little River
2
Lily Pond
Dykes Pond
School St.
TO BOSTON (35 MILES) 128
Magnolia Ave.
4
127
Western Ave.
TO SALEM 3
127
Manchester by-the-Sea
Magnolia
5 Mussel Point
Manchester Harbor
Raymond St.
Hesperus Ave.
Singing Beach
Magnolia Harbor

Listed by Site Number

1	Castle Hill/Crane's Beach	3	Trask House
2	Essex Shipbuilding Museum	4	Ravenswood Park
		5	Hammond Castle
		6	Beauport Museum

7 Rocky Neck Art Colony
8 Gloucester Stage Company

Listed Alphabetically

Bearskin Neck, 15. Rockport

Beauport Museum, 6. 75 Eastern Point Rd, Gloucester ☎ 978/283-0800

Cape Ann Historical Society, 11. 27 Pleasant St, Gloucester ☎ 978/283-0455

Castle Hill/Crane's Beach, 1. 200 Argilla Rd, Ipswich ☎ 978/356-4354

Chamber Music Festival, 14. performs at 12 Main St (Rockport Art Assn), Rockport ☎ 978/546-7391

Essex Shipbuilding Museum, 2. 28 Main St, Essex ☎ 978/768-7541

Fishermen's Memorial, 9. Stacy Blvd, Gloucester

Gloucester Stage Co, 8. 267 E Main St, Gloucester ☎ 978/281-4099

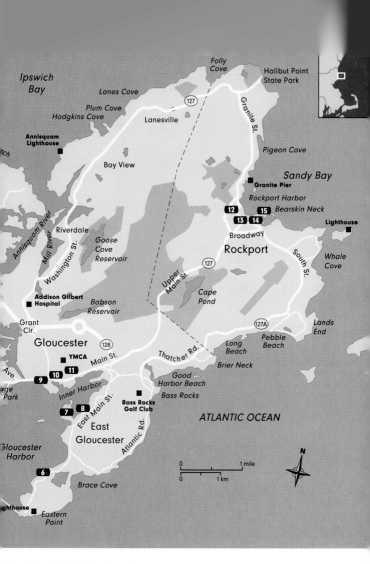

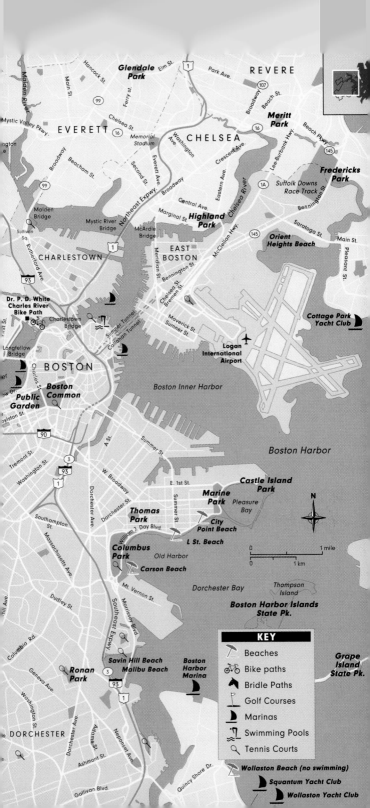

Glendale Park — Elm St. — Park Ave. — REVERE

Hancock St. — Main St. — 99 — Ferry St. — Chelsea St. — 1

107 — Beach St. — Broadway

EVERETT — 16 — Memorial Stadium — Second St. — Washington Ave. — CHELSEA — Meritt Park — 16 — Lee-Burbank Hwy. — Beach Pkwy. — 145

Mystic Valley Pkwy. — Broadway — Beacham St. — Everett Ave. — Broadway — Central Ave. — Crescent Ave. — Eastern Ave. — Chelsea River — Fredericks Park — Bennington St.

Malden Bridge — Mystic River Bridge — McArdle Bridge — Marginal St. — Highland Park — 1A — Suffolk Downs Race Track — Saratoga St.

Sullivan Sq. — 93 — Rutherford Ave. — CHARLESTOWN — Meridian St. — EAST BOSTON — Bennington St. — McClellan Hwy. — 145 — Orient Heights Beach — Main St. — Pleasant St.

Dr. P. D. White Charles River Bike Path — Charlestown Bridge — Chelsea St. — Brenton St. — Cottage Park Yacht Club

Longfellow Bridge — Sumner Tunnel — Callahan Tunnel — Maverick St. — Sumner St. — Logan International Airport

BOSTON — Charles St. — Boston Common — Boston Inner Harbor

Public Garden — Boylston St. — 90 — A St. — Summer St. — Boston Harbor

Tremont St. — Washington St. — 3 — 93 — 1 — Dorchester Ave. — W. Broadway — E. 1st St. — Summer St. — Castle Island Park — N

Southampton St. — Massachusetts Ave. — Dorchester Ave. — Marine Park — Pleasure Bay — Thomas Park — City Point Beach — L St. Beach

Dudley St. — Columbus Park — Old Harbor — Carson Beach — 0 — 1 mile — 0 — 1 km

Mt. Vernon St. — Dorchester Bay — Thompson Island — Boston Harbor Islands State Pk.

Columbia Rd. — Geneva Ave. — Ronan Park — Savin Hill Beach — Malibu Beach — Boston Harbor Marina — Grape Island State Pk.

DORCHESTER — Dudley St. — Southeast Expwy. — Morrissey Blvd. — 3 — 93 — 1 — Neponset Ave. — Adams St.

Ashmont St. — Gallivan Blvd. — Quincy Shore Dr. — Wollaston Beach (no swimming)

Squantum Yacht Club — Wollaston Yacht Club

KEY

- ⚓ Beaches
- 🚲 Bike paths
- 🐎 Bridle Paths
- ⛳ Golf Courses
- 🌙 Marinas
- 〰️ Swimming Pools
- 🔍 Tennis Courts

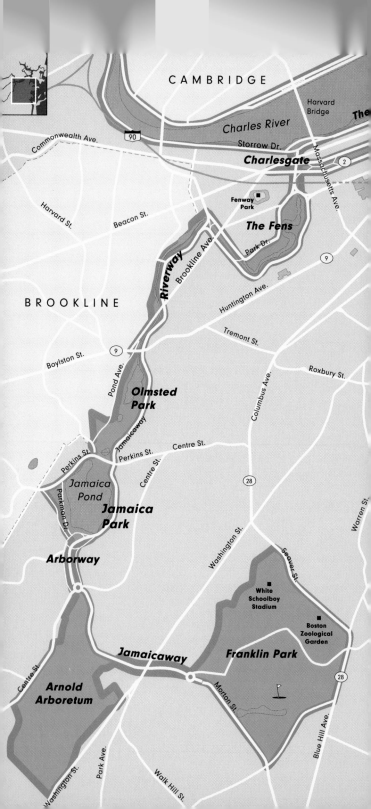

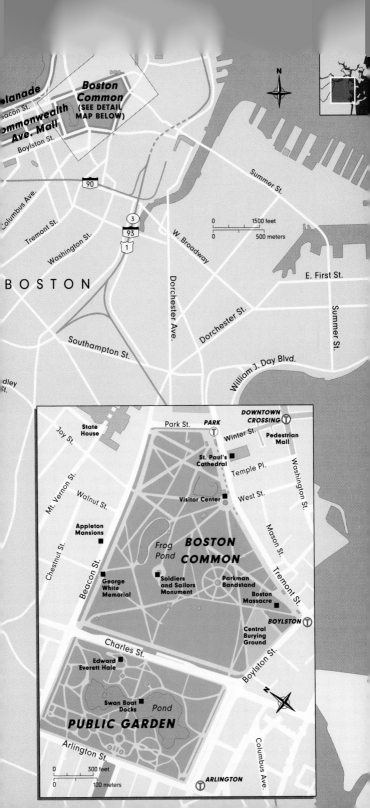

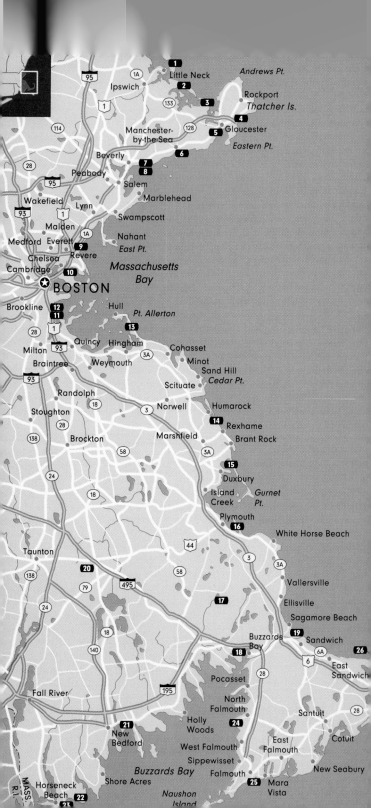

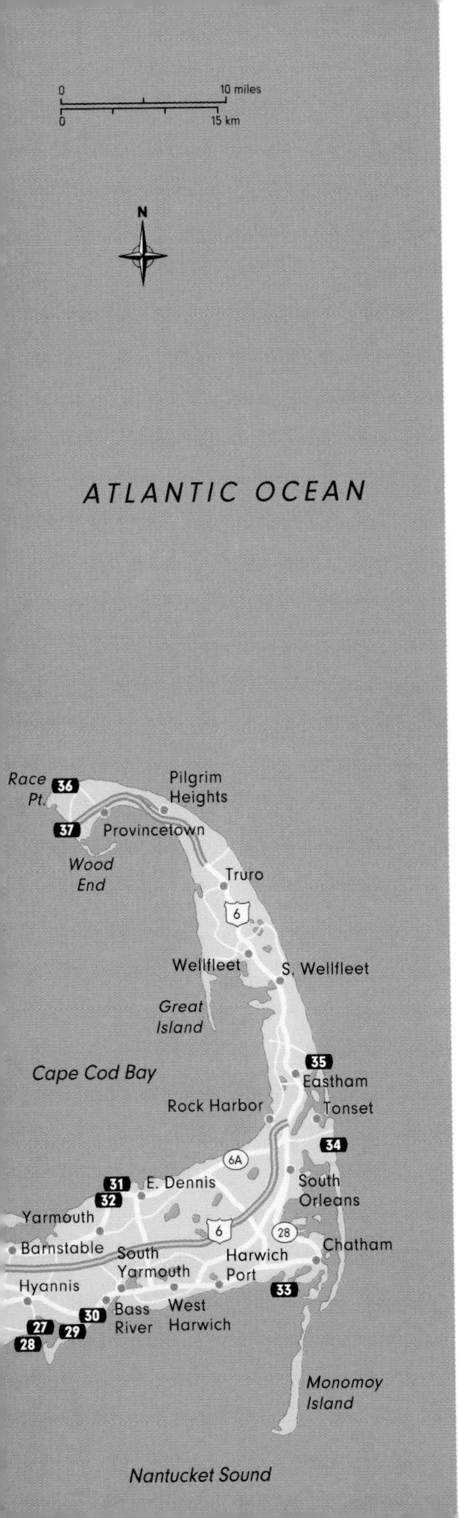

0
10 miles
0
15 km
N
ATLANTIC OCEAN
Race Pt.
36
Pilgrim Heights
37
Provincetown
Wood End
Truro
6
Wellfleet
S. Wellfleet
Great Island
Cape Cod Bay
35
Eastham
Rock Harbor
Tonset
34
6A
31
E. Dennis
32
South Orleans
Yarmouth
6
28
Barnstable
South Yarmouth
Harwich Port
Chatham
Hyannis
33
30
Bass River
West Harwich
27
29
28
Monomoy Island
Nantucket Sound

Listed by Site Number

NORTH SHORE

1 Plum Island
2 Crane's Beach
3 Wingaersheek
4 Good Harbor
5 Cressy Beach
6 Singing Beach
7 Dane St
8 Lynch Park

GREATER BOSTON

9 Revere Beach
10 Constitution Beach
11 Malibu Beach
12 Savin Hill Beach

SOUTH SHORE

13 Nantasket Beach
14 Humarock Beach
15 Duxbury Beach
16 Plymouth Beach
17 College/Fearing Ponds
18 Onset Beach
19 Scusset Beach

BRISTOL COUNTY

20 Massasoit State Park
21 Fort Phoenix State Park
22 Demarest Lloyd State Park
23 Horseneck Beach

CAPE COD

24 Old Silver
25 Surf Drive
26 Sandy Neck
27 Kalmus Park
28 Orrin Keyes
29 Sea Gull
30 Bass River Beach
31 Corporation Rd Beach
32 Mayflower Beach
33 Harding's Beach
34 Nauset Beach
35 Coast Guard Beach
36 Race Point
37 Herring Cove

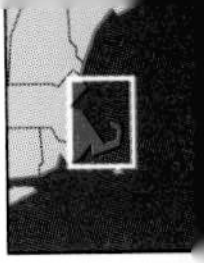

Listed Alphabetically

NORTH SHORE

Crane's Beach, 2. Ipswich
☎ 508/356-4354. *R,L,F,P*

Cressy Beach, 5. Stage Fort Pk,
Gloucester ☎ 978/281-9790. *R*

Dane St, 7. Beverly
☎ 978/921-6067. *R,L,P*

Good Harbor, 4. Thatcher Rd,
Gloucester ☎ 978/281-9790. *R,L,F,P*

Lynch Park, 8. Ober St, Beverly
☎ 978/921-6067. *L,P*

Plum Island, 1. Newburyport
☎ 978/462-6680. *R,L*

Singing Beach, 6.
Manchester-by-the-Sea. *R,L*

Wingaersheek, 3. Concord St,
Gloucester ☎ 978/281-9790. *R,L,F,P*

GREATER BOSTON

Constitution Beach, 10. E Boston
☎ 727-5114. *R,L,F,P*

Malibu Beach, 11. Dorchester
☎ 727-5114. *R,L,F,P*

Revere Beach, 9. Rt IA,
Revere ☎ 781/286-8190. *R,L,F,P*

Savin Hill Beach, 12.
Dorchester ☎ 727-5114. *R,L,F,P*

SOUTH SHORE

College/Fearing Ponds, 17.
Plymouth ☎ 508/866-2526. *R,P*

Duxbury Beach, 15. Duxbury
☎ 781/934-6586. *R,L,F,P*

Humarock Beach, 14. Marshfield
☎ 781/545-8740. *R,L*

Nantasket Beach, 13. Hull
☎ 781/925-2000. *R,L,F,P*

Onset Beach, 18. Wareham
☎ 508/291-3101. *F,P*

Plymouth Beach, 16. Plymouth
☎ 508/830-4095. *L,F,P*

Scusset Beach, 19. Bourne
☎ 508/888-0859. *R,F,P*

BRISTOL COUNTY

Demarest Lloyd State Park, 22.
Dartmouth ☎ 508/636-3298. *R,L*

Fort Phoenix State Park, 21.
Fairhaven ☎ 508/992-4524. *R,L*

Horseneck Beach, 23. Westport
☎ 508/636-8816. *R,L*

Massasoit State Park, 20. E Taunton
☎ 508/822-7405. *R,L*

CAPE COD

Bass River Beach, 30. So Shore Dr,
Yarmouth ☎ 508/398-2231. *R,F,P*

Coast Guard Beach, 35.
Rt 6, Eastham ☎ 508/255-3421. *R,F,P*

Corporation Rd Beach, 31.
Rt 6A, Dennis ☎ 508/394-8300. *R,F,P*

Harding's Beach, 33. Rt 28,
W Chatham ☎ 508/945-5158. *R,F*

Herring Cove, 37. Rt 6, Provincetown
☎ 508/487-7097. *R,F,P*

Kalmus Park, 27. Ocean St, Hyannis
☎ 508/790-6345. *R,F,P*

Orrin Keyes, 28. Sea St, Hyannis
☎ 508/790-6345. *R,F,P*

Mayflower Beach, 32. Rt 6A, Dennis
☎ 508/394-8300. *R,F,P*

Nauset Beach, 34. Rt 28, E Orleans
☎ 508/240-3785. *R,F,P*

Old Silver, 24. Quaker Rd,
No Falmouth ☎ 508/457-2567. *R,F,P*

Race Point, 36. Rt 6, Provincetown
☎ 508/487-7097. *R*

Sandy Neck, 26. Rt 6A, W Barnstable
☎ 508/790-6345. *R,F,P*

Sea Gull, 29. South Sea Ave,
W Yarmouth ☎ 508/398-2231. *R,F,P*

Surf Drive, 25. Surf Dr, Falmouth
☎ 508/457-2567. *R,F,P*

*Note: Hours for lifeguards and
refreshments are limited; call
to check.*

R=Restrooms L=Lifeguard F=Food P=Parking

Martha's Vineyard & Nantucket

MAP 40

Martha's Vineyard

TO FALMOUTH

TO WOODS HOLE

TO NEW BEDFORD

TO WOODS HOLE

TO HYANNIS

Vineyard Sound

West Chop Lighthouse

Owen Park Beach

East Chop Lighthouse

Tisbury Town Beach

Nantucket Sound

Lake Tashmoo

Vineyard Haven

Oak Bluffs

TO NANTUCKET

Lambert's Cove

Oak Bluffs Beach

Cedar Tree Neck

Cape Poge Wildlife Refuge & Lighthouse

Joseph Sylvia State Beach

Cape Poge

Indian Hill Rd.

Lambert's Cove Rd.

State Rd.

Old County Rd.

Edgartown-Vineyard Haven Rd.

County Rd.

N.Y. Ave.

Sengekontacket Pond

State Beach

Cape Poge Bay

Edgartown Lighthouse

Dyke Rd.

CORELLUS STATE FOREST

Airport

STATE FOREST

Chappaquiddick Island

East Beach

West Tisbury

Edgartown

Wasque Reserv.

North Rd.

Middle Rd.

South Rd.

Edgartown-West Tisbury Rd.

Airport Rd.

Katama Rd.

Katama Bay

Menemsha Hills Reservation

Tisbury Great Pond

Edgartown Great Pond

Wasque Point

Gay Head Lighthouse

Menemsha Beach

Menemsha

Chilmark

Long Point

Katama (South Beach)

Gay Head Cliffs

South Rd.

Menemsha Pond

Moshup Beach

Squibnocket Pond

Lucy Vincent Beach (restricted)

Squibnocket Beach (restricted)

KEY

🏖 Beaches

🚲 Bike Paths

ATLANTIC OCEAN

Martha's Vineyard

Nantucket

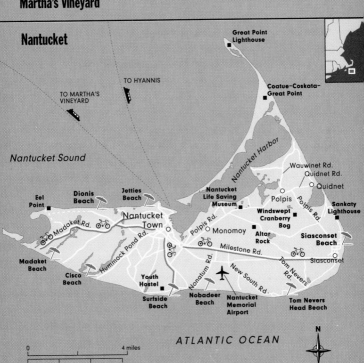

Great Point Lighthouse

TO HYANNIS

Coatue-Coskata-Great Point

TO MARTHA'S VINEYARD

Nantucket Sound

Nantucket Harbor

Wauwinet Rd.

Quidnet Rd.

Quidnet

Eel Point

Dionis Beach

Jetties Beach

Nantucket Life Saving Museum

Polpis

Sankaty Lighthouse

Madaket Rd.

Nantucket Town

Polpis Rd.

Windswept Cranberry Bog

Polpis Rd.

Monomoy

Altar Rock

Siasconset Beach

Madaket Beach

Hummock Pond Rd.

Polpis Rd.

Milestone Rd.

Siasconset

Cisco Beach

Youth Hostel

Nonamut Rd.

New South Rd.

Tom Nevers Rd.

Surfside Beach

Nobadeer Beach

Nantucket Memorial Airport

Tom Nevers Head Beach

ATLANTIC OCEAN

Foxboro Access

Dorchest
B

BOSTON

95
128
1
28

Needham

135

27   16

EXIT 17

EXIT 16   Dedham

EXIT 15   Milton

Islington

EXIT 1   28

Westwood   EXIT 2   EXIT 4
EXIT 21

Holliston   109

1A   95   Canton   24

115   Medfield   Norwood   EXIT 2

Millis   1

27   Walpole   EXIT 10   27

N   EXIT 9

Norfolk   Sharon   Stoughton

115   Foxboro
Stadium   EXIT 8   EXIT 18

Franklin   1A   138

EXIT 17   140   Foxboro   EXIT 17

495   Wrentham   95   24

121   EXIT 15   EXIT 14   EXIT 7   Easton

EXIT 6
EXIT 13   106   EXIT 16

R.I.   Mansfield

0 ____ 4 miles
0 ____ 6 km

Foxboro Stadium

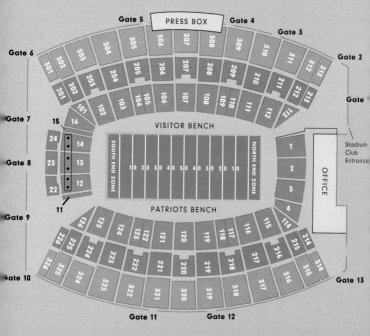

Gate 5   PRESS BOX   Gate 4

Gate 6   305 304 306 307 308 309   Gate 3

301 302 303 204 205 206 207 208 209 310 311 312 313   Gate 2

201 202 203 104 105 106 107 108 109 110 210 211 212 213   Gate

Gate 7   101 102 103   111 112 213

15 16   VISITOR BENCH   Gate 2

Gate 7   24 14   Stadium
Club
Gate 8   23 13   1   Entrance

22 12   SOUTH END ZONE   10 20 30 40 50 40 30 20 10   NORTH END ZONE   2   OFFICE

11   3

Gate 9   PATRIOTS BENCH   4

Gate 10   126 125 124 123 122 121 120 119 118 117 116 115 114   214 215

226 225 224 223 222 221 220 219 218 217 216   216

326 325 324 323 322 321 320 319 318 317 315 314   Gate 13

Gate 11   Gate 12

FleetCenter

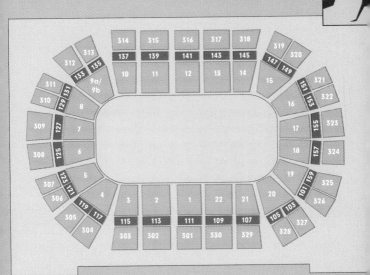

314	315	316	317	318	319	320
137	139	141	143	145	147 149	

313
312
133 135
311 129 131
310
309 127
308 125
307 123
306 121
305 119 117
304

9a/9b
10 11 12 13 14 15
8
7
6
5
4
3 2 1 22 21 20
115 113 111 109 107
303 302 301 330 329

321
322
323
324
325
326
327
328

16
17
18
19
151 153
155
151
101 159
105 103

NORTH STATION Causeway Street

N

Fenway Park

Brookline Ave.

Lansdowne Street

Gate E

Gate C

Gate A

33
32
31
30
29
28
27
26
25
24
23
22
21
20
19 18 17 16 15 14 13 12 11 10 9 8 7 6 5
34 35 36 37 38 39 40 41 42 43 1 2 3 4

Bleachers

ROOF BOX SEATS

Field Box Seats
Box Seats
Grandstand/Reserved
Roof Box Seats

Gate

Yawkey Way

Gate D Van Ness Street N

Parking

Parking

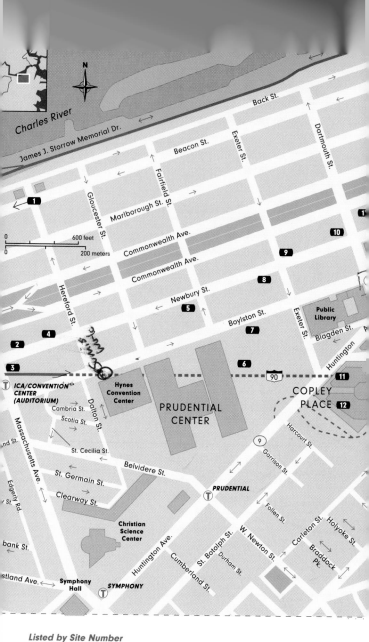

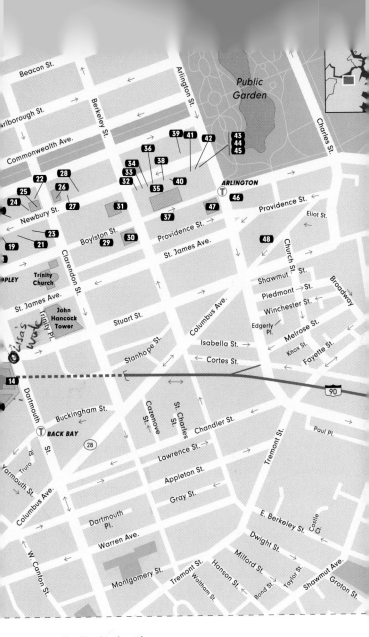

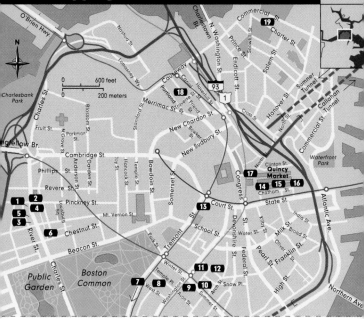

Listed by Site Number

1 Helen's Leather Shop	**7** Freedburg of Boston	**14** Coach
2 Boston Antiques Coop	**8** Brattle Book Shop	**15** Crate & Barrel
3 James Billings Antiques	**9** Macy's	**16** Brookstone
4 The Designers	**10** Long's Jewelers	**17** Signature
5 Charles St Flowers	**11** Filene's	**18** Hilton's Tent City
6 Kennedy Studio	**12** London Harness Co	**19** D'hajj
	13 Eric Fuchs	

Listed Alphabetically

Boston Antiques Coop, 2.
119 Charles St ☎ 227-9810

Brattle Book Shop, 8. 9 West St
☎ 542-0210

Brookstone, 16. Quincy Market
☎ 439-4460

Charles Street Flowers, 5.
115 Charles St ☎ 742-0499

Coach, 14. Quincy Market ☎ 723-1777

Crate & Barrel, 15. Quincy Market
☎ 742-6025

The Designers, 4. 106 Charles St
☎ 720-3967

D'hajj, 19. 502 Commercial St
☎ 367-1287

Eric Fuchs, 13. 28 Tremont St
☎ 227-7935

Filene's, 11. 426 Washington St
☎ 357-2100

Freedburg of Boston, 7.
112 Shawmut Ave ☎ 357-8600

Helen's Leather Shop, 1.
110 Charles St ☎ 742-2077

Hilton's Tent City, 18. 272 Friend St
☎ 227-9242

James Billings Antiques, 3.
34 Charles St ☎ 367-9533

Kennedy Studio, 6. 31 Charles St
☎ 523-9868

London Harness Co, 12.
60 Franklin St ☎ 542-9234

Long's Jewelers, 10. 40 Summer St
☎ 426-8500

Macy's, 9. 450 Washington St
☎ 357-3000

Signature, 17. Dock Square
☎ 227-4885

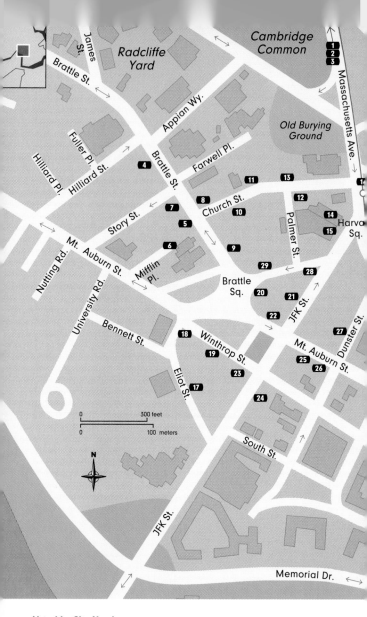

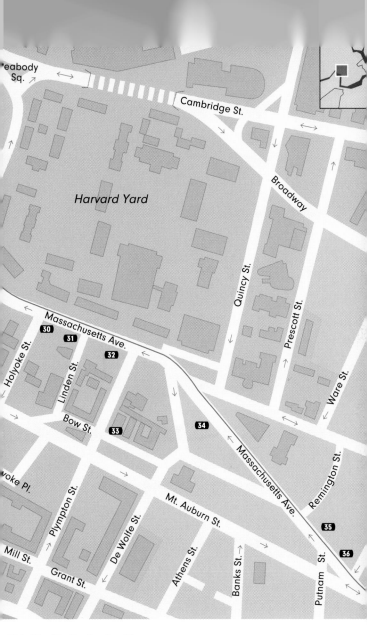

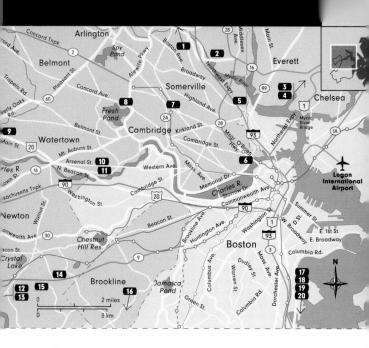

SOMERVILLE

North End

Old North Church

Joy St.
Linwood St.
Ward St.
South St.
Porter St.
St.
Medford St.
28

Cambridge St.
Prospect St.
Tremont St.
Hampshire St.
Norfolk St.
Harvard St.
Washington St.
Allen Dr.
Massachusetts Ave.
Landsdowne St.
Albany St.

Prince St.
134
133
Hull St.
Snowhill St.
Sheafe St.
Salem St.
Charter St.
Unity St.
Tileston St.
N. Bennet St.
Battery St.
Salutation St.
Hanover Ave.
Murphy Ct.
Harris St.
Clark St.
112
111
110
132
Lombard Pl.
Thatcher St.
Margaret St.
Noyes Pl.
Baldwin Pl.
Prince St.
113
Fleet St.
North St.
Commercial St.
109
Endicott St.
Margin St.
Lynn St.
Cooper St.
130
108
118
115
114
116
119
117
Lewis St.
Sun Ct.
107
106
104
Stillman St.
127
125
120
Garden Ct.
Morton St.
129
131
126
121
105
Cross St.
128
123
122
Fulton St.
Richmond St.
103
102
HAYMARKET
Fitzgerald Expwy.
124
Summer Tunnel
Commercial St.
Commercial Wharf N.
Blackstone St.
I-93
North St.
Callahan Tunnel
101
New Sudbury St.
Congress St.
Hanover St.
Union St.
Creek Sq.
Salt La.
99
100
98
Clinton St.
Waterfront Park

Briggs Field (MIT)

Charles River

Memorial Dr.
Harvard Br.
James J. Storrow Memorial Drive
Back St.
Dartmouth St.
Marlborough St.
Beacon St.
Hereford St.
Gloucester St.
Fairfield St.
Exeter St.
Clarendon St.
1
2
3
Back St.
Bay State Rd.
4
5
6
7
20
Kenmore Sq.
Beacon St.
Newbury St.
Charlesgate W.
Charlesgate E.
Commonwealth Ave.
27
26
25
24
28
17
22
34
Newbury St.
23
18
20
21
Boylston St.
19
Blagden St.
33
36
Ipswich St.
Dalton St.
29
90
30
31
32
12
15
37
Prudential Center
16
9
Copley Place
Fenway Park
Yawkey Way
Brookline Ave.
Lansdowne St.
Ness St.
Ipswich St.
Van
Boylston St.
Peterborough St.
Kilmarnock St.
Queensberry St.
Park Dr.
14
Belvidere St.
10
Christian Science Center
Burbank St.
13
Westland Ave.
Symphony Hall
Back Bay Fens Park
Agassiz Rd.
St. Stephen St.
Gainsborough St.
Huntington Ave.
St. Botolph St.
Carleton St.
Columbus Ave.
Warren Ave.
11
Wellington St.
W. Newton Sq.
W. Rutland Sq.
Concord St.
Rutland St.
W. Springfield St.
Camden St.
Museum of Fine Arts
Louis Prang St.
Museum Rd.
Forsyth Way
Forsyth St.
Hemenway St.
9
Northeastern University
Parker St.
Ruggles St.
Columbus Ave.
Tremont St.
Lenox St.
Shawmut Ave.
Kendall St.
Washington St.
8

0   1200 feet
0   400 meters

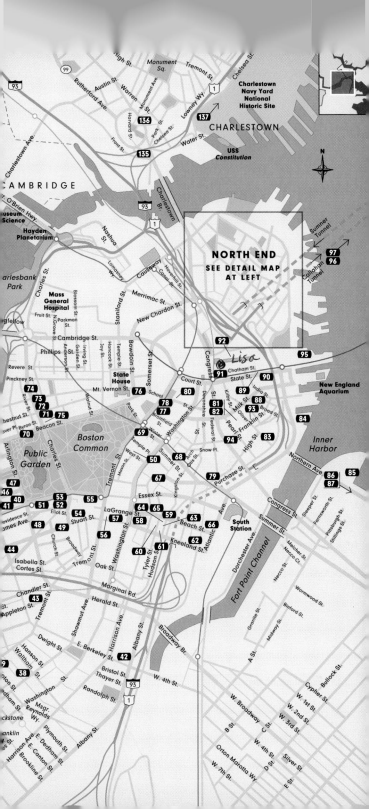

$$$$ = over $35 $$$ = $25–$35 $$ = $15–$25 $ = under $15
Based on cost per person, excluding drinks, service, and 5% sales tax.

Listed Alphabetically (cont.)

Famous Atlantic Fish Co., 34.
777 Boylston Ave ☎ 242-2229.
Pizza/Pasta. $

Felicia's, 122. 145A Richmond St
☎ 523-9885. Italian. $$

Figs, 71. 42 Charles St
☎ 227-1777. Pizza/Pasta. $

Figs, 136. 67 Main St, Charlestown
☎ 242-2229. Pizza/Pasta. $

Filippo, 134. 283 Causeway
☎ 742-4143. Italian. $$

Five North Square, 107. 5 North Sq
☎ 720-1050. Italian. $$$

Florence's, 105. 190 North St
☎ 523-4480. Italian. $$

Florentine Café, 114. 333 Hanover St
☎ 227-1777. Italian. $$$

Fratelli Pugliuca's, 126. 14 Parmenter
St ☎ 367-1504. Italian. $$

Giacomo's, 115. 355 Hanover St
☎ 523-9026. Italian. $$

Golden Palace, 61. 14 Tyler St
☎ 423-4565. Chinese. $$

Grand Chau Chow, 65. 45 Beach St
☎ 292-5166. Chinese. $

Grill 23, 44. 161 Berkeley St
☎ 542-2255. Steak. $$$$

G'Vanni's, 117. 2 Prince St
☎ 523-0107. Italian. $$

Gyuhama, 21. 827 Boylston St
☎ 437-0188. Japanese. $$$

Hamersley's Bistro, 39. 553 Tremont St
☎ 423-2700. Eclectic/French. $$$$

Hard Rock Cafe, 36. 131 Clarendon St
☎ 424-7625. American. $$

Ho Yuen Ting, 63. 13A Hudson St
☎ 426-2316. Chinese/Seafood. $$

House of Siam, 31. 21 Huntington Ave
☎ 267-1755. Thai. $

Hungry I, 74. 7½ Charles St
☎ 227-3524. American. $$$

Icarus, 43. 3 Appleton St
☎ 426-1790. American. $$$$

Il Panino, 93. 295 Franklin St
☎ 338-1000. Italian. $$

Imperial Seafood, 59. 70 Beach St
☎ 426-8543. Chinese/Dim Sum. $$

J.C. Hillary's, 34. 793 Boylston St
☎ 536-6300. American. $$

Jacob Wirth, 57. 31 Stuart St
☎ 338-8586. German. $$

Jae's Cafe, 11. 520 Columbus Ave
☎ 421-9405. Korean. $$

Jimmy's Harborside, 87.
242 Northern Ave ☎ 423-1000.
Seafood. $$$

Joseph's Aquarium, 100. 101 Atlantic
Ave ☎ 523-4000. Seafood. $$$

Julien, 82. Hotel Meridien, 250
Franklin St ☎ 451-1900. French. $$$$

Kyoto, 49. 201 Stuart St
☎ 542-1166. Steak. $$$

La Summa, 109. 30 Fleet St
☎ 523-9503. Italian. $$

Legal Sea Foods, 48.
Park Plaza ☎ 426-4444. Seafood. $$$

L'Espalier, 17. 30 Gloucester St
☎ 262-3023. French. $$$$

Les Zygomates, 66. 129 South St
☎ 542-5108. French Bistro. $$$

**Library Grill at Hampshire
House, 85.** 84 Beacon St
☎ 227-9600. American. $$$

Locke-Ober Cafe, 69. 3 Winter Pl
☎ 542-1340. American. $$$$

L'Osteria, 127. 109 Salem St
☎ 723-7847. Italian. $$

Maison Robert, 80. 45 School St
☎ 227-3370. French. $$$$

Mamma Maria, 106. 3 North Sq
☎ 523-0077. Italian. $$$$

Marketplace Café, 92. Quincy
Market ☎ 227-1272. American. $$

Massimino's, 133. 207 Endicott St
☎ 523-5959. Italian. $$

Mateo's, 116. 351 Hanover St
☎ 523-9265. Italian. $$

Medieval Manor, 42. 246 E Berkeley
St ☎ 423-4900. Dinner Theater. $$$

Mercury Bar, 55. 116 Boylston St
☎ 482-7799. Eclectic. $$$

Michael's Waterfront, 102.
85 Atlantic Ave ☎ 367-6425.
Steak/Seafood. $$$

Miyako, 20. 279A Newbury St
☎ 236-0222. Japanese. $$

Montien, 56. 63 Stuart St
☎ 367-2353. Thai. $$

Morton's of Chicago, 24. 1 Exeter Pl
☎ 266-5858. Steak. $$$$

Mother Anna's, 124. 211 Hanover St
☎ 523-8496. Italian. $$

Nara, 83. 85 Wendell St
☎ 338-5395. Japanese/Korean. $$

Nicole, 128. 54 Salem St
☎ 742-6999. Italian. $$

No Name, 85. 15 ½ Fish Pier, off
Northern Ave ☎ 338-7539.
Seafood. $$

Oasis Cafe, 132. 176 Endicott St
☎ 523-9274. American. $$

Olives, 135. 10 City Sq,
Charlestown ☎ 242-1999.
Italian/Mediterranean. $$$

On the Park, 38. 315 Shawmut Ave
☎ 426-0862. American. $$

Papa Razzi, 28. 271 Dartmouth St
☎ 536-9200. Italian/Med. $$$

Paramount Steakhouse, 73.
44 Charles St ☎ 523-8832.
American/Greek. $

Parish Café, 41. 361 Boylston St
☎ 247-4777. American. $

Parker's, 78. Omni Parker House
☎ 227-8600. American. $$$$

Pat's Pushcart, 129. 61 Endicott St
☎ 523-9616. Italian. $$

Pho Pasteur, 58. 8 Kneeland St
☎ 451-0247. Vietnamese. $

Piccolo Nido, 104. 247 North St
☎ 742-4272. Italian. $$

Plaza Dining Room, 33. Copley Pl
☎ 267-5300. Continental. $$$$

Pomodoro, 118. 319 Hanover St
☎ 367-4348. Italian. $$

Providence, 3. 1223 Beacon St,
Brookline ☎ 232-0300. Italian. $$$

Rattlesnake Bar & Grill, 40.
384 Boylston St ☎ 859-8555.
American. $

Rebecca's, 75. 21 Charles St
☎ 742-9747. American. $$

Ristorante Lucia, 111. 415 Hanover St
☎ 367-2353. Italian. $$$

Ristorante Saraceno, 125. 286
Hanover St ☎ 227-5888. Italian. $$$

Ristorante Toscano, 72. 41 Charles St
☎ 723-4090. Italian. $$$

Rita's Place, 137. 88 Winnisimmet St,
Chelsea ☎ 884-9010. Italian. $$$

Ritz-Carlton, 47. 15 Arlington St
☎ 536-5700. American. $$$

Rowes Wharf Restaurant, 84.
Boston Harbor Hotel, Atlantic Ave
☎ 439-3995. Seafood. $$$$

Sablone's, 96. 107A Porter St
☎ 567-8140. Italian. $$$

Sakura-bana, 88. 57 Broad St
☎ 542-4311. Japanese. $$

Schroeder's, 79. 8 High St
☎ 426-1234. Continental. $$$

Scullers Grille, 2. Doubletree
Hotel ☎ 783-0090. American. $$$

Seasons, 98. Bostonian Hotel
☎ 523-3600. Continental. $$$$

Skipjack's, 35. 199 Clarendon St
☎ 536-3500. Seafood. $$$

Small Planet, 30. 565 Boylston St
☎ 536-4477. International. $

Sol Azteca, 6. 914A Beacon St,
Brookline ☎ 262-0909. Mexican. $$

Sonsie, 19. 327 Newbury St
☎ 351-2500. International. $$

Spasso, 27. 160 Commonwealth Ave
☎ 536-8656. Italian. $$$

Sports Depot, 1. 353 Cambridge St,
Allston ☎ 783-2300. American. $$

Stephanie's on Newbury, 25. 190
Newbury St ☎ 236-0990. American. $$$

Tatsukichi, 90. 189 State St
☎ 720-2468. Japanese. $$$

Terramia, 131. 98 Salem St
☎ 523-3112. Italian. $$$

Thai Cuisine, 13. 14A Westland Ave
☎ 262-1485. Thai. $$

Top of the Hub, 37. Prudential Ctr
☎ 536-1775. American. $$$$

Trattoria a Scalinatella, 121. 255
Hanover St ☎ 742-8240. Italian. $$$

Trident Booksellers & Café, 19.
338 Newbury St ☎ 267-8688. Café. $

Turner Fisheries, 32. Westin Hotel,
10 Huntington Ave ☎ 424-7425 $$$

29 Newbury, 46. 29 Newbury St
☎ 536-0290. American. $$$

Union Oyster House, 99. 41 Union St
☎ 227-2750. Seafood/Raw Bar. $$

Veronique, 5. 20 Chapel St, Brookline
☎ 731-4800. French. $$$

Villa Francesca, 123. 150 Richmond St
☎ 367-2948. Italian. $$

Village Fish, 4. 22 Harvard St,
Brookline ☎ 566-3474. Seafood. $$

Zuma's Tex-Mex Cafe, 92. Quincy
Mkt ☎ 367-9114. Tex-Mex. $$$

$$$$ = *over $35* $$$ = *$25–$35* $$ = *$15–$25* $ = *under $15*
Based on cost per person, excluding drinks, service, and 5% sales tax.

Listed Alphabetically

Algiers Café, 11. Brattle Thtre, ☎ 492-1557. Middle Eastern. $

Anago Bistro, 41. 798 Main St ☎ 876-8444. American/European. $$$

Bartley's Burger Cottage, 22. 1246 Mass Ave ☎ 354-6559. Burgers. $

Bertucci's, 8. 21 Brattle St ☎ 864-4748. Pizza. $

Bisuteki, 28. 777 Memorial Drive ☎ 492-7777. Japanese/Steak. $$

Blue Room, 42. 1 Kendall Square ☎ 494-9034. Eclectic. $$$

Boca Grande, 45. 149 First St ☎ 354-5550. Mexican. $

The Border Cafe, 14. 32 Church St ☎ 864-6100. Mexican/Cajun. $$

Cafe Celador, 7. 5 Craigie Cir ☎ 661-4073. French. $$$

Cafe Sushi, 23. 1105 Mass Ave ☎ 492-0434. Japanese. $$

California Pizza Kitchen, 10. 16-18 Eliot St ☎ 492-0006. Pizza/Amer. $$

Casa Mexico, 18. 75 Winthrop St ☎ 491-4552. Mexican. $$

Casa Portugal, 34. 1200 Cambridge St ☎ 491-8880. Portuguese. $$

Casablanca, 12. 40 Brattle St ☎ 876-0999. Seafood/Pasta. $$

Changsho, 4. 1712 Mass Ave ☎ 547-6565. Mandarin/Szechuan. $$

Chez Henri, 6. 1 Shepard St ☎ 354-8980. French. $$$

Chez Nous, 10. 147 Huron Ave ☎ 864-6670. French. $$$$

Cottonwood Cafe, 3. 1815 Mass Ave ☎ 661-7440. Southwestern. $$

Daddy O's Bohemian Cafe, 35. 134 Hampshire St ☎ 354-8371. Eclectic. $

Dali, 29. 415 Washington St, Som ☎ 661-3254. Spanish. $$$

Dionysos, 27. 777 Memorial Dr ☎ 661-6800. Greek. $$

Druid, 31. 1357 Cambridge St ☎ 497-0965. Irish. $

East Coast Grill, 32. 1271 Cambridge St ☎ 491-6568. BBQ/Seafood. $$$

8 Holyoke St, 20. 8 Holyoke St ☎ 497-5300. Mediterranean. $$$$

Elephant Walk, 47. Union Sq, Som ☎ 623-9939. French/Asian. $$$

Forest Cafe, 5. 1682 Mass Ave ☎ 661-7810. Mexican. $$

Green St Grill, 39. 280 Green St ☎ 876-1655. Caribbean. $$

Grendel's Den, 16. 89 Winthrop St ☎ 491-1160. American. $$

Harvest, 13. 44 Brattle St ☎ 492-1115. American. $$$

Henrietta's Table, 33. Charles Hotel Hvd Sq ☎ 661-5005. American. $$

India Pavilion, 37. 17 Central Sq ☎ 547-7463. Indian. $$

Iruna, 17. 56 JFK St ☎ 868-5633. Spanish. $$

John Harvard's Brew House, 19. 33 Dunster St ☎ 868-3585. American. $$

La Groceria, 40. 853 Main St ☎ 547-9258. Italian. $$

Magnolia's, 33. 1193 Cambridge St ☎ 576-1971. Cajun. $$

Pampas, 26. 928 Mass Ave ☎ 661-6613. Brazilian. $$

Poppa & Goose, 46. 69 First St ☎ 497-6772. Asian. $$

Porterhouse Cafe, 2. 2046 Mass Ave ☎ 354-9793. BBQ. $$

Redbones, 1. 55 Chester St, Som ☎ 225-2121. BBQ/Southern $$

Rialto, 15. Charles Hotel Harvard Sq ☎ 661-5050. American. $$$$

Roka, 24. 1001 Mass Ave ☎ 661-0344. Japanese. $$

S&S Deli, 30. 1334 Cambridge St ☎ 354-0620. Deli. $

Salamander, 44. 1 Athenaeum St ☎ 225-2121. New American. $$$$

Shalimar of India, 38. 546 Mass Ave ☎ 547-9280. Indian. $$

Spinnaker Italia, 43. Hyatt Regency Hotel ☎ 492-1234. Italian. $$$

Sunset Cafe, 36. 851 Cambridge St ☎ 547-2938. Portuguese. $$

Tandoor House, 25. 991 Mass Ave ☎ 661-9001. Indian. $$

Tealuxe, 9. Zero Brattle St ☎ 441-0077. Tearoom. $

Upstairs at the Pudding, 21. 10 Holyoke St ☎ 864-1933. Cont. $$$

$$$$ = over $35 $$$ = $25-$35 $$ = $15-$25 $ = under $15
Based on cost per person, excluding drinks, service, and 5% sales tax.

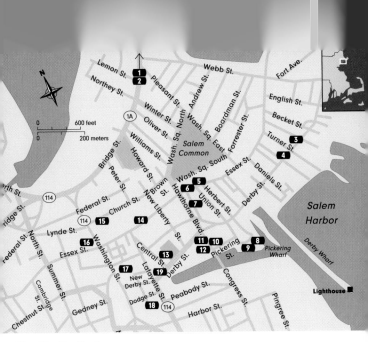

Listed by Site Number

1 Texas Red's BBQ	8 Victoria Station	14 Thai Place
2 Stromberg's	9 Chase House	15 Lyceum
3 Derby Fish & Lobster	10 Asahi	16 Red Raven's Havana
4 In a Pig's Eye	11 Grapevine	17 Lobster Shanty
5 Café de LaRosa	12 Red Raven's	18 Dodge St Grill
6 Nathaniel's	Love Noodle	19 Salem Beer Works
7 Oh Calcutta	13 Roosevelt's	

Listed Alphabetically

Asahi, 10. 21 Congress St
☎ 978/744-5376. Japanese. $$

Café de LaRosa, 5. 107 Essex St
☎ 978/741-4088. Italian. $$$

Chase House, 9. Pickering Wharf
☎ 978/744-0000. Seafood. $$

Derby Fish & Lobster, 3. 215 Derby St
☎ 978/745-2064. Seafood. $$

Dodge St Grill, 18. 7 Dodge St
☎ 978/745-0139. American. $$

Grapevine, 11. 26 Congress St
☎ 978/745-9335. American/Italian. $$

In a Pig's Eye, 4. 148 Derby St
☎ 978/741-4436. American. $$

Lobster Shanty, 17. Salem Mktpl
☎ 978/745-7449. American. $$

Lyceum, 15. 43 Church St
☎ 978/745-7665. Continental. $$

Nathaniel's, 6. Hawthorne Inn Hotel
☎ 978/744-4080. American. $$$

Oh Calcutta, 7. 6 Hawthorne Blvd
☎ 978/744-6570. Indian. $$

Red Raven's Havana, 16. 90
Washington St ☎ 978/740-3888.
Eclectic. $$

Red Raven's Love Noodle, 12.
75 Congress St ☎ 978/745-8558.
Eclectic. $$

Roosevelt's, 13. 300 Derby St
☎ 978/745-9608. American. $$

Salem Beer Works, 19. 278 Derby St
☎ 978/745-2337. Microbrewery. $$

Stromberg's, 2. 2 Bridge St
☎ 978/744-1863. Seafood/Amer. $$

Texas Red's BBQ, 1. 29 Bridge St
☎ 978/744-7777. BBQ. $$

Thai Place, 14. Museum Place Mall
☎ 978/741-8008. Thai. $$

Victoria Station, 8. Pickering Wharf
☎ 978/745-3400. American. $$

$$$$ = over $35 $$$ = $25-$35 $$ = $15-$25 $ = under $15
Based on cost per person, excluding drinks, service, and 5% sales tax.

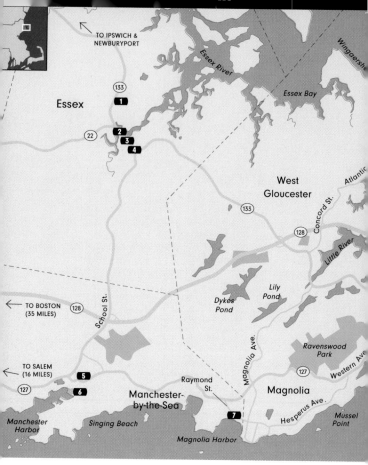

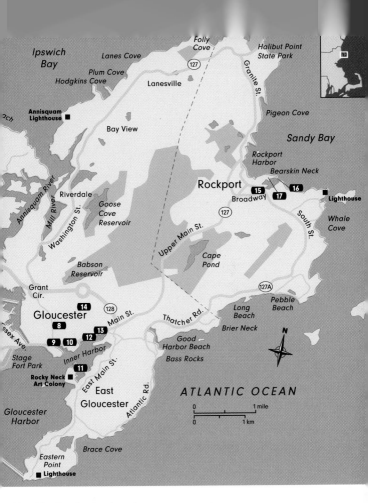

Lighthouse

Ipswich Bay

Lanes Cove

Folly Cove

Halibut Point State Park

Plum Cove
Hodgkins Cove

Granite St.

Lanesville

127

Annisquam Lighthouse

Pigeon Cove

Bay View

Sandy Bay

Rockport Harbor

Bearskin Neck

Rockport

15 **16**

17

Broadway

Lighthouse

South St.

Whale Cove

Riverdale

Mill River

Washington St.

Goose Cove Reservoir

Upper Main St.

Cape Pond

127

Babson Reservoir

Grant Cir.

14 128

8

Gloucester

Main St.

Thatcher Rd.

Pebble Beach

127A

Long Beach

13

9 **10** **12**

Brier Neck

Good Harbor Beach

Bass Rocks

11

Inner Harbor

Stage Fort Park

Essex Ave.

Rocky Neck Art Colony

East Main St.

East Gloucester

Atlantic Rd.

ATLANTIC OCEAN

N

Gloucester Harbor

0   1 mile
0   1 km

Brace Cove

Eastern Point
Lighthouse

$$$$ = over $35 $$$ = $25-$35 $$ = $15-$25 $ = under $15
Based on cost per person, excluding drinks, service, and 5% sales tax.

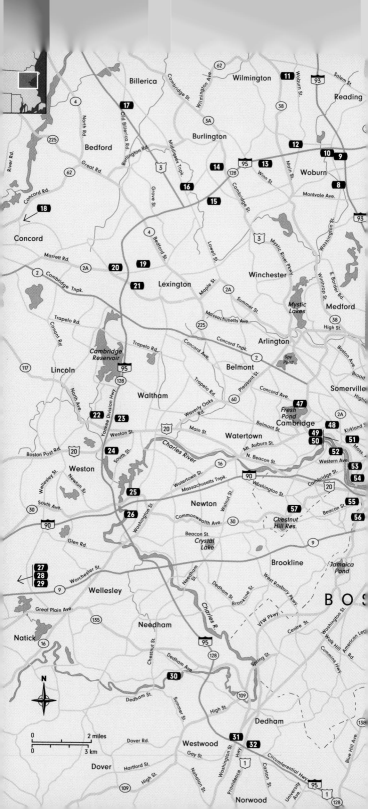

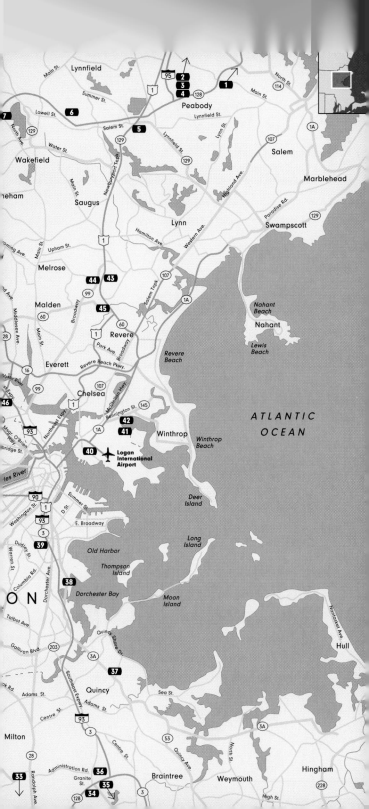

Listed by Site Number

1 Quality Inn
2 Comfort Inn
3 Marriott Peabody
4 Tara Ferncroft
5 Holiday Inn
6 Hilton Colonial
7 Best Western Lord Wakefield
8 HoJo Woburn
9 Holiday Inn Crowne Plaza
10 Hampton Inn
11 Red Roof Inn
12 Courtyard Marriott
13 Ramada Woburn
14 Marriott Burlington
15 Wyndham Burlington
16 HoJo Burlington
17 Renaissance Bedford Hotel
18 Best Western Conc
19 Holiday Inn Express

20 Sheraton Lexington
21 Battle Green Inn
22 Doubletree Guest Suites Waltham
23 Best Western East
24 Westin Waltham
25 Marriott Newton
26 Holiday Inn Newton
27 Holiday Inn Crowne Plaza
28 Travelodge Natick
29 Sheraton Tara
30 Inn on the Square
31 Holiday Inn
32 Comfort Inn Dedham
33 Holiday Inn
34 Sheraton Tara
35 Motel 6
36 Days Inn Braintree
37 Best Western Adams Inn
38 Suisse Chalets
39 South Bay Hotel

40 Harborside Hyatt
41 Airport Ramada
42 Holiday Inn Airport
43 HoJo Revere
44 Days Inn Saugus
45 Town Line Inn
46 Holiday Inn
47 Best Western Homestead
48 Sheraton Commander
49 Charles Hotel
50 Harvard Sq Hotel
51 Inn at Harvard
52 Doubletree Guest Suites Hotel
53 HoJo Cambridge
54 Hyatt Regency
55 Holiday Inn
56 Best Western Inn at Children's
57 Best Western Terrace

Listed Alphabetically

Airport Ramada, 41. Logan Airport
☎ 569-9300. 🖷 567-1947. $$$

Battle Green Inn, 21. 1720 Mass Ave, Lexington ☎ 781/862-6100. $

Best Western Adams Inn, 37.
29 Hancock St, Quincy
☎ 328-1500. 🖷 328-3067. $

Best Western Concord, 18.
740 Elm St, Concord
☎ 978/369-6100. 🖷 978/371-1656. $

Best Western East, 23.
477 Totten Pd Rd, Waltham
☎ 781/890-7800. 🖷 781/890-4937. $

Best Western Homestead, 47.
220 Alewife Brook Pkwy, Cambridge
☎ 491-1890. 🖷 491-4932. $$

Best Western Inn at Children's, 56.
342 Longwood Ave
☎ 731-4700. 🖷 731-6273. $$

Best Western Lord Wakefield, 7.
595 North Ave, Wakefield
☎ 781/245-6100. 🖷 781/245-2904. $

Best Western Terrace Motor Lodge, 57. 1650 Commonwealth Ave, Brighton ☎ 566-6260. 🖷 731-3543. $

Charles Hotel, 49. 1 Bennett Sq, Cam
☎ 864-1200. 🖷 864-5715. $$$$

Comfort Inn, 2. 50 Dayton St, Danvers
☎ 978/777-1700. 🖷 978/777-4647. $

Comfort Inn Dedham, 32.
235 Elm St, Dedham
☎ 781/326-6700. 🖷 781/326-9264. $

Courtyard Marriott Woburn, 12.
240 Mishawum Rd, Woburn
☎ 781/932-3200. 🖷 781/935-6163. $$

Days Inn Braintree, 36.
190 Wood Rd, Braintree ☎ 848-1260.
🖷 848-9799. $

Days Inn Saugus, 44. Rt 1, Saugus
☎ 781/233-1800. 🖷 781/233-1814. $

Doubletree Guest Suites Hotel, 52.
400 Soldiers Field Rd
☎ 783-0090. 🖷 783-0897. $$$

Doubletree Guest Suites Waltham, 22.
550 Winter St, Waltham
☎ 781/890-6767. 🖷 781/890-8197. $$$

Hampton Inn Woburn, 10.
315 Mishawum Rd, Woburn
☎ 781/935-7666. 🖷 781/933-6899. $$

Harborside Hyatt, 40. 101 Harborside Dr, Logan Airport ☎ 568-1234.
🖷 567-8856. $$$$

Harvard Sq Hotel, 50.
110 Mt Auburn St, Cambridge
☎ 864-5200. 🖷 864-2409. $$$

Hilton Colonial, 6. Rt 128, Wakefield
☎ 781/245-9300. 📠 781/245-0842. $$$

Holiday Inn, 55. 1200 Beacon St,
Brookline ☎ 277-1200. 📠 734-6991. $$

Holiday Inn, 31. Rts 1 & 128, Dedham
☎ 781/329-1000. 📠 781/329-0903. $$

Holiday Inn, 5. Rt 1, Peabody
☎ 978/535-4600. 📠 978/535-8238. $$

Holiday Inn, 33. 1374 N Main St,
Randolph ☎ 781/961-1000.
📠 781/963-0089. $$

Holiday Inn, 46. 30 Washington St,
Som ☎ 628-1000. 📠 628-0143. $$$

Holiday Inn Airport, 42. Rt 1A,
E Boston ☎ 569-5250. 📠 569-5159. $$$

Holiday Inn Crowne Plaza, 27.
1360 Worcester Rd, Natick
☎ 508/653-8800. 📠 508/653-1708. $$$

Holiday Inn Crowne Plaza, 9.
2 Forbes Rd, Woburn
☎ 781/932-0999. 📠 781/932-0903. $$$

Holiday Inn Express, 19.
440 Bedford St, Lexington
☎ 781/861-0850. 📠 781/861-0821. $$

Holiday Inn Newton, 26.
399 Grove St, Newton
☎ 969-5300. 📠 965-4280. $$

Howard Johnson's Burlington, 16.
Rt 128, Burlington ☎ 781/272-6550.
📠 781/229-8164. $

Howard Johnson's Cambridge, 53.
777 Memorial Dr, Cambridge
☎ 492-7777. 📠 492-6038. $$$

Howard Johnson's Revere, 43.
407 Squire Rd, Revere
☎ 781/284-7200. 📠 781/289-3176. $

Howard Johnson's Woburn, 8.
Montvale Ave, Woburn
☎ 781/935-8160. 📠 781/932-9623. $

Hyatt Regency, 54.
575 Memorial Dr, Cambridge
☎ 492-1234. 📠 491-6906. $$$$

Inn at Harvard, 51. 1201 Mass Ave,
Cam ☎ 491-2222. 📠 491-6520. $$$$

Inn on the Square, 30.
576 Washington St, Wellesley
☎ 781/235-0180. 📠 781/235-5263. $$

Marriott Burlington, 14.
Rts 128 & 3A, Burlington
☎ 781/229-6565. 📠 781/630-3523. $$$

Marriott Newton, 25.
Commonwealth Ave, Newton
☎ 969-1000. 📠 527-6914. $$$

Marriott Peabody, 3. Rt 128,
Peabody ☎ 978/977-9700.
📠 978/977-0297. $$

Motel 6, 35. 125 Union St, Braintree
☎ 781/848-7890. $

Quality Inn, 1. Rt 128, Danvers
☎ 978/774-6800. 📠 978/774-6502. $$$

Ramada Woburn, 13.
Rts 38 & 128, Woburn
☎ 781/935-8760. 📠 781/938-1790. $$

Red Roof Inn Woburn, 11.
19 Commerce Way, Woburn
☎ 781/935-7110. 📠 781/932-0657. $

Renaissance Bedford, 17.
44 Middlesex Tnpk, Bedford
☎ 781/275-5500. 📠 781/276-7527. $$$

Sheraton Commander, 48.
16 Garden St, Cambridge
☎ 547-4800. 📠 868-8322. $$$

Sheraton Lexington, 20.
727 Marrett Rd, Lexington
☎ 781/862-8700. 📠 781/863-0404. $$$

Sheraton Tara, 34.
37 Forbes St, Braintree
☎ 781/848-0600. 📠 781/843-9492. $$$

Sheraton Tara, 29.
1657 Worcester Rd, Framingham
☎ 508/879-7200. 📠 508/875-7593. $$$

South Bay Hotel, 39.
5 Howard Johnson Plaza, Dorchester
☎ 288-3030. 📠 265-6543. $

Suisse Chalets, 38.
800 & 900 Morrissey Blvd
☎ 287-9100, 287-9200.
📠 265-9287, 282-2365. $

Tara Ferncroft, 4.
Ferncroft Rd, Danvers
☎ 978/777-2500. 📠 978/750-7959. $$$

Town Line Inn, 45. Rt 1, Malden
☎ 781/324-7400. 📠 781/397-8501. $$

Travelodge Natick, 28.
1350 Worcester Rd, Natick
☎ 508/655-2222. 📠 508/655-7953. $

Westin Waltham, 24. 70 Third Ave,
Waltham ☎ 781/290-5600.
📠 781/290-5636. $$$$

Wyndham Inn Burlington, 15.
Wheeler Rd, Burlington ☎ 781/272-
8800. 📠 781/221-4605. $$

$$$$ = over $190 $$$ = $130-$190 $$ = $100-$130 $ = under $100
Prices are for a standard double room, excluding 9.7% room tax.

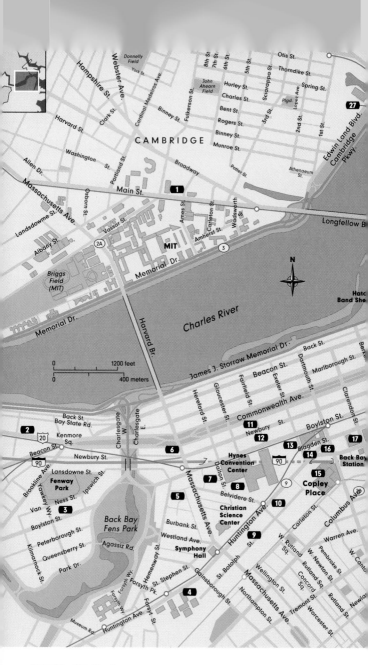

Listed Alphabetically

Back Bay Hilton, 7.
40 Dalton St
☎ 236-1100. 📠 867-6139. $$$

Beacon Inns & Guesthouses, 12.
248 Newbury St
☎ 266-7142. 📠 266-7276. $

Berkeley Residence Club (Women), 19. 40 Berkeley St
☎ 482-8850. 📠 424-6558. $

Boston Harbor Hotel, 32.
70 Rowes Wharf
☎ 439-7000. 📠 345-6799. $$$$

Boston International Hostel, 5.
12 Hemenway St
☎ 536-9455. 📠 424-6558. $

Boston Park Plaza Hotel & Towers, 22. 64 Arlington St
☎ 426-2000. 📠 423-1708. $$$$

The Bostonian, 29.
Faneuil Hall Marketplace
☎ 523-3600. 📠 523-2454. $$$$

Cambridge Center Marriott, 1.
2 Cambridge Center
☎ 494-6600 📠 494-0036. $$$

Chandler Inn Hotel, 18.
26 Chandler St
☎ 482-3450. 📠 542-3428. $

The Colonnade, 10.
120 Huntington Ave
☎ 424-7000. 📠 424-1717. $$$

Copley Plaza, 17. Copley Sq
☎ 267-5300. 📠 267-7668. $$$$

Copley Square, 14.
47 Huntington Ave
☎ 536-9000. 📠 267-3547. $$

Eliot Hotel, 6.
370 Commonwealth Ave
☎ 267-1607. 📠 536-9114. $$

Four Seasons, 24. 200 Boylston St
☎ 338-4400. 📠 423-0154. $$$$

Greater Boston YMCA, 4.
316 Huntington Ave ☎ 536-7800. $

Holiday Inn-Government Center, 26. 5 Blossom St
☎ 742-7630. 📠 742-4192. $$

Howard Johnson's Fenway, 3.
1271 Boylston St
☎ 267-8300. 📠 267-2763. $$

Howard Johnson's Kenmore Sq, 2.
575 Commonwealth Ave
☎ 267-3100. 📠 424-1045. $$

Le Meridien, 30. 250 Franklin St
☎ 451-1900. 📠 423-2844. $$$$

Lenox Hotel, 13. 710 Boylston St
☎ 536-5300. 📠 236-0351. $$$$

Marriott Copley Place, 15.
110 Huntington Ave
☎ 236-5800. 📠 236-5885. $$$$

Marriott Long Wharf, 31. 296 State St
☎ 227-0800. 📠 227-2867. $$$$

Midtown Hotel, 9.
220 Huntington Ave
☎ 262-1000. 📠 262-8739. $$

Newbury Guest House, 11.
261 Newbury St
☎ 437-7666. 📠 262-4243. $

Omni Parker House, 28. 60 School St
☎ 227-8600. 📠 742-5729. $$$

Radisson, 21. 200 Stuart St
☎ 482-0242. $$

Ritz-Carlton, 23. 15 Arlington St
☎ 536-5700. 📠 536-1335. $$$$

Royal Sonesta, 27.
5 Cambridge Pkwy
☎ 491-3600. 📠 661-5956. $$$

Sheraton Boston Hotel & Towers, 8.
39 Dalton St
☎ 236-2000. 📠 236-6095. $$$

Swissôtel, 25. 1 Ave de Lafayette
☎ 451-2600. $$$$

Tremont House, 20. 275 Tremont St
☎ 426-1400. 📠 338-7881. $$

Westin, 16. 10 Huntington Ave
☎ 262-9600. 📠 424-7502. $$$$

$$$$ = over $190 $$$ = $130–$190 $$ = $100–$130 $ = under $100
Prices are for a standard double room, excluding 9.7% tax and service charges.

MAP 53 Performing Arts/Downtown

Listed by Site Number

1 Tsai Ctr/Boston Univ	**5** Huntington Theatre Co	**8** ICA Theater
2 Boston Children's Theatre	**6** Boston Pops	**9** Hynes Auditorium
3 Boston Conservatory Theater	**6** Boston Symphony	**10** New Theater
	6 Handel & Haydn Soc	**11** Boston Camerata
4 Jordan Hall/NE Conservatory	**6** Symphony Hall	**11** Lyric Stage
	7 Berklee Perf Center	**12** City Stage Company

Listed Alphabetically

Berklee Performance Ctr, 7.
136 Mass Ave ☎ 266-7455

Boston Ballet, 15. Wang Ctr,
270 Tremont St ☎ 695-6950

Boston Camerata, 11.
140 Clarendon St ☎ 262-2092

Boston Center for the Arts (BCA), 13.
539 Tremont St ☎ 426-5000

Boston Chamber Music Society, 22.
286 Congress St ☎ 422-0086

Boston Children's Theatre, 2.
93 Mass Ave ☎ 424-6634

Boston Conservatory Theater, 3.
8 The Fenway ☎ 536-6340

Boston Lyric Opera, 18.
Emerson Majestic Theatre ☎ 542-4912

Boston Pops, 6.
Symphony Hall ☎ 266-1492

Boston Symphony Orchestra, 6.
Symphony Hall ☎ 266-2378

Charles Playhouse, 14.
74 Warrenton St ☎ 426-6912

City Stage Co, 12.
551 Tremont St ☎ 542-2291

Colonial Theatre, 19.
106 Boylston St ☎ 426-9366

Emerson Majestic Theatre, 18.
219 Tremont St ☎ 578-8727

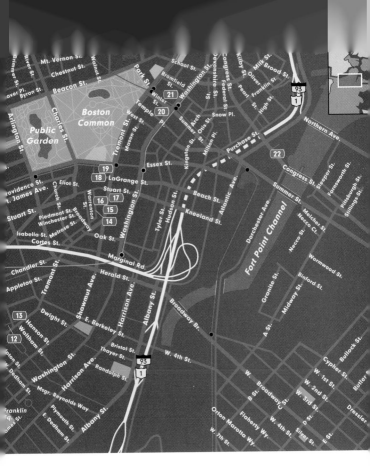

Listed by Site Number

Listed Alphabetically

COMMERCIAL FILMS

Allston Cinemas, 16.
214 Harvard Ave ☎ 277-2140

Arlington Capitol Theater, 1.
204 Mass Ave ☎ 781/648-4340

Belmont Studio Cinema, 2.
376 Trapelo Rd ☎ 484-1706

Braintree 10, 45. off Forbes Rd
☎ 781/848-1070

Brattle Theater, 6. Brattle St,
Cambridge ☎ 876-6837

Brockton Westgate 7, 47.
Rt 27 ☎ 508/588-5050

Burlington 10, 34. Rt 128, exit 32B
☎ 781/229-9200

Cheri, 23. 50 Dalton St
☎ 536-2870

Chestnut Hill General Cinema, 14.
27 Boylston St ☎ 277-2500

Cleveland Circle, 15. Cleveland
Circle, Brookline ☎ 566-4040

Coolidge Corner Cinema, 18.
Coolidge Cnr, Brookline ☎ 734-2500

Copley Place, 24.
100 Huntington Ave ☎ 266-1300

Danvers 6, 32. Rt 128, exit 24
☎ 978/777-2555

Danvers Liberty Tree Mall, 31.
Liberty Tree Mall ☎ 978/777-1818

Dedham Community Theatre, 41.
580 High St ☎ 781/326-1463

Dedham Showcase, 42. 950
Providence Hwy (Rt 1) ☎ 781/326-4955

Framingham 14, 38.
Rt 9 ☎ 508/628-4404

Fresh Pond Cinema, 3. Fresh Pond
Plaza, Cambridge ☎ 661-2900

Harborlight Mall Cinema, 46.
Rt 3A, No Weymouth ☎ 781/864-4580

Harvard Square Theater, 7.
10 Church St, Cambridge ☎ 864-4580

Janus Theater, 9.
57 JFK St, Cambridge ☎ 661-3737

Lexington Flick, 36.
1794 Mass Ave ☎ 781/861-6161

Natick Sony, 39.
Rt 9 ☎ 508/237-5840

Nickelodeon, 20.
606 Commonwealth Ave ☎ 424-1500

North Shore General Cinema, 33.
Rt 128, Peabody ☎ 978/599-1310

Quincy Showcase, 44.
1585 Hancock St ☎ 773-5700

Revere Showcase, 37.
Rt 1 & Squire Rd ☎ 781/286-1660

Somerville Theater, 4.
55 Davis Sq ☎ 625-5700

Somerville Sony, 5.
Assembly Sq Mall ☎ 628-7000

West Newton Cinema, 13.
1296 Washington St ☎ 964-6060

Woburn Showcase, 35.
Rts 128 & 38 ☎ 781/933-5330

ART FILMS/SPECIAL PROGRAMS

Boston Public Library, 25.
666 Boylston St ☎ 536-5400

Boston Univ/Sherman Union, 19.
771 Commonwealth Ave ☎ 353-2169

Brighton Branch Library, 12.
40 Academy Hill Rd ☎ 782-6032

Brookline Public Library, 17.
361 Washington St ☎ 730-2345

Central Square Library, 10.
45 Pearl St, Cambridge ☎ 349-4010

Codman Square Library, 43. 690
Washington St, Dorchester ☎ 436-8214

French Library, 27.
53 Marlborough St ☎ 266-4351

Goethe Institute, 26.
170 Beacon St ☎ 262-6050

Harvard Film Archive, 8.
24 Quincy St, Cambridge ☎ 495-4700

Institute of Contemporary Art, 22.
955 Boylston St ☎ 266-5152

Museum of Fine Arts, 21.
465 Huntington Ave ☎ 267-9300

Museum of Science, 28.
Science Park ☎ 723-2500

Newton Free Library, 11.
414 Centre St, Newton Ctr ☎ 552-7145

North End Branch Library, 29.
25 Parmenter St ☎ 227-8135

South Boston Branch Library, 30.
646 E Broadway ☎ 268-0180

Wellesley Free Library, 40.
530 Washington St ☎ 781/431-7813

MAP 55 Nightlife/Cambridge & Somerville

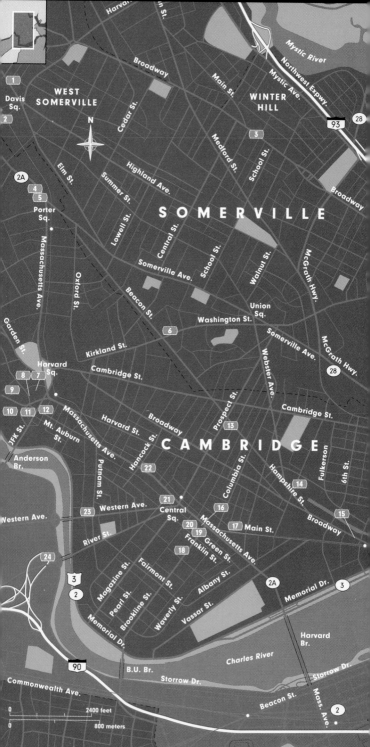

1	Johnny D's	**11**	House of Blues	**19**	TT The Bear's
2	Somerville Theater	**12**	John Harvard's Brew House	**20**	Middle East
3	Willow			**21**	Cantab Lounge
4	Finnegan's Wake	**13**	Ryles	**22**	Plough & Stars
5	Toad	**14**	Kendall Café	**23**	Western Front
6	Kirkland Café	**15**	Cambridge Brewing Co	**24**	Scullers
7	Passim	**16**	Phoenix Landing		
8	Black Rose	**17**	Small Planet		
9	Cafe Algiers	**18**	Man Ray		
10	Regattabar				

Brew Moon, 8.
50 Church St, Cam
☎ 499-2739. Brewpub/DJ

Cafe Algiers, 9.
40 Brattle St, Cam
☎ 492-1557. Coffeehouse

Cambridge Brewing Co, 15.
I Kendall Square, Cam
☎ 494-1994. Live Varied Music

Cantab Lounge, 21.
738 Mass Ave, Cam
☎ 354-2685. Live Rock/Blues

Finnegans' Wake, 4.
2067 Mass Ave, Cam
☎ 576-2240. Live Music

House of Blues, 11.
96 Winthrop St, Cam
☎ 491-2583. Blues

John Harvard's Brew House, 12.
33 Dunster St, Cam
☎ 868-3585. Live Music/Bar

Johnny D's, 1.
I7 Holland St, Som
☎ 776-2004. Live Varied Music

Kendall Café, 14.
233 Cardinal Medeiros Way, Cam
☎ 661-0993. Live Acoustic Music

Kirkland Café, 6.
425 Washington St, Som
☎ 491-9640. Rock

ManRay, 18.
2I Brookline St, Cam
☎ 864-0400. Alternative

Middle East, 20.
472 Mass Ave, Cam
☎ 492-5162. Live Varied Music

Passim, 7.
47 Palmer St, Cam
☎ 492-7679. Live Folk/Acoustic

Phoenix Landing, 16.
5I2 Mass Ave, Cam
☎ 576-6260. Live Music

Plough & Stars, 22.
9I2 Mass Ave, Cam
☎ 441-3455. Live Rock/Blues

Regattabar, 10.
Charles Hotel, Cam
☎ 876-7777. Live Jazz

Ryles, 13.
2I2 Hampshire St, Cam
☎ 876-9330. Live Jazz

Scullers, 24.
Doubletree Guest Suites,
400 Soldiers Field Rd, Allston
☎ 783-0090. Live Jazz

Small Planet Bar & Grill, 17.
795 Main St, Cam
☎ 441-9020. Live Music

Somerville Theater, 2.
Davis Sq, Som
☎ 625-5700. Live Music

Toad, 5.
I9I2 Mass Ave, Cam
☎ 497-4950. Live Varied Music

T.T. The Bear's, 19.
I0 Brookline St, Cam
☎ 492-0080. Live Music

Western Front, 23.
343 Western Ave, Cam
☎ 492-7772. Live Varied Music

Willow Jazz Club, 3.
699 Broadway, Som
☎ 623-9874. Live Jazz

MAP **56** **Nightlife/Boston**

Kenmore Square & Lansdowne Street

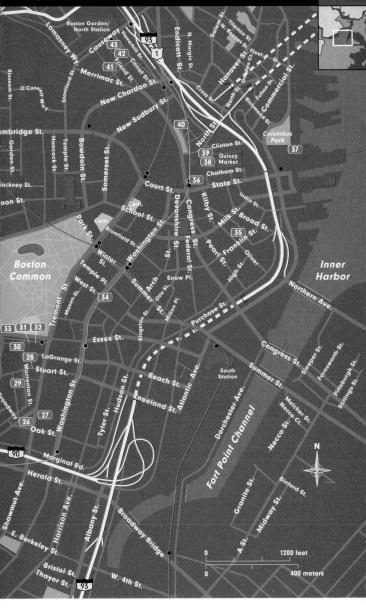

MAP 56

Listed Alphabetically

Alley Cat, 30.
1 Boylston Place ☎ 351-2510. DJ

Avalon, 10.
15 Lansdowne St ☎ 262-2424.
Dancing/Live Music

Avenue C, 31. 120 Boylston St
☎ 423-3832. Club/Alternative

Axis, 9. 13 Lansdowne St
☎ 262-2437. Club/Varied Music

Back Bay Brewing Co., 18.
755 Boylston St ☎ 424-8300. Brewery

Bill's Bar, 7. 5½ Lansdowne St
☎ 421-9678. Bar/Live Music

Boston Beer Works, 5.
61 Brookline Ave ☎ 536-2337. Brewery

Brew Moon, 28. 115 Stuart St
☎ 523-6467. Brew Pub

Bull & Finch Pub, 25.
Hampshire House, 84 Beacon St
☎ 227-9605. Bar/Live Music

Cask & Flagon, 3. 62 Brookline Ave
☎ 536-4840. Classic Rock

Chaps, 19. 27 Huntington Ave
☎ 266-7778. Dancing/Gay

Claddagh, 20. 335 Columbus Ave
☎ 262-9874. Live Music

Club Cafe, 22. 209 Columbus Ave
☎ 536-0966. Cabaret/Gay

Comedy Connection, 38.
Quincy Market ☎ 248-9700. Comedy

Commonwealth Brewing Co, 41.
138 Portland St ☎ 523-8383.
Brewery/Live Music

Copperfields, 2. 98 Brookline Ave
☎ 247-8605. Live Music

Daisy Buchanan's, 17.
240A Newbury St ☎ 247-8516. Bar/DJ

Dick Doherty's Comedy Vault, 32.
124 Boylston St ☎ 729-2565. Comedy

Harp, 43. 85 Causeway St
☎ 742-1010. Rock/Dancing

Harper's Ferry, 1. 158 Brighton Ave,
Allston ☎ 254-9743. Live Music

Houlihan's, 36. 60 State St
☎ 367-6377. Dancing/DJ

Il Panino, 35. 295 Franklin St
☎ 338-1000. Dancing

Irish Embassy Pub, 42.
234 Friend St ☎ 742-6618. Live Music

Jake Ivory's, 3. 1 Lansdowne St
☎ 247-1222. Dueling Pianos

Jillians, 11. 145 Ipswich St
☎ 437-0300. Pool/Billiards

Joy Boston, 34. 533 Washington St
☎ 338-6999. Dancing

Karma Club, 4. 9 Lansdowne St
☎ 421-9595. Live Music

Local 186, 12. 186 Harvard Ave,
Allston ☎ 351-2660. Rock/Reggae

Mama Kin, 8. 36 Lansdowne St
☎ 536-2100. Live Music

Marketplace Cafe, 39. Quincy
Market ☎ 227-9660. Live Music

Mercury Bar, 33. 116 Boylston St
☎ 482-7799. DJ

Napoleon Club, 23.
52 Piedmont St
☎ 338-7547. Piano Bar/Gay

Nick's Comedy Stop, 29.
100 Warrenton St
☎ 482-0930. Comedy

NYC Jukebox, 26. 275 Tremont St
☎ 542-1123. Dancing/DJ

Paradise, 13. 967 Commonwealth
Ave ☎ 562-8804. Live Music

Purple Shamrock, 40. 1 Union St
☎ 227-2060. Bar/Varied Music

Rathskeller (The Rat), 6.
528 Commonwealth Ave
☎ 536-2750. Live Rock

Ritz-Carlton Bar, 24.
15 Arlington St ☎ 536-5700. Bar

The Roxy, 27. 279 Tremont St
☎ 338-7699. Live Music/Dancing

The Spot, 14. 1270 Boylston St
☎ 424-7747. Dancing/Gay/Straight

Tia's, 37. Marriott Long Wharf
☎ 227-0828. Outdoor Bar

Top of the Hub, 15. Prudential
Center ☎ 536-1775. Bar

Turner Fisheries, 21.
Westin Hotel, 10 Huntington Ave
☎ 262-9600. Live Jazz

Waves, 37. Marriott Long Wharf
☎ 227-0800. Dancing/DJ

Zachary's, 16. Colonnade Hotel
☎ 424-7000. Live Jazz

Zanzibar, 30. 1 Boylston Place
☎ 351-7000. Dancing/DJ